EMILY SHEEHAN is an award-winning writer, podcaster and dramaturg. In 2023, the critically-acclaimed world premiere of her play *Monument* at Red Stitch Actors' Theatre, directed by Artistic Director Ella Caldwell, enjoyed an extended sold-out season, a return season by popular demand in 2024, followed by a national tour in 2025. Her latest play *Frame Narrative* opened Lucy Clements' inaugural 2024 season as Artistic Director of the The Old Fitz's New Ghosts Theatre Company and enjoyed multiple 5, 4.5 and 4 star reviews. Her other plays include *Hell's Canyon* (Old 505 Theatre / La Mama Theatre/ Regional Arts Victoria / Vimeo on Demand film of stage play), *Daisy Moon Was Born This Way* (Q Theatre) and *Versions Of Us* (Canberra Youth Theatre). Her plays have been developed through Melbourne Theatre Company's Cybec Electric, Red Stitch INK, Playwriting Australia National Script Workshops and New Ghosts Theatre Company. Playwriting awards include the Rodney Seaborn Playwrights' Award (Winner), Victorian Premier's Literary Awards (Finalist), The Patrick White Playwrights' Award (Finalist), Max Afford Playwrights' Award (Finalist), UK's Theatre503 Playwriting Award (Longlist) and Melbourne Fringe Festival Award (Winner). Emily has completed dramaturgy attachments with The Bush Theatre (London), Traverse Theatre (Edinburgh) and Playwrights' Studio Scotland and worked as a dramaturg for Theatre503 (London), Arts Centre Melbourne and the Victorian College of the Arts. She has also undertaken dramaturgy observations with the National Theatre of Scotland and Melbourne Theatre Company, and worked as a script reader for Playwriting Australia and Currency Press. Emily currently hosts the *Playwright's Process Podcast*, a monthly podcast about writing craft and the creative process. She teaches Playwriting at the Victorian College of the Arts, University of Melbourne.

FRAME NARRATIVE

EMILY SHEEHAN

CURRENCY PRESS
The performing arts publisher

CURRENCY PLAYS

First published in 2025
by Currency Press Pty Ltd,
Gadigal Land, Suite 310, 46—56 Kippax Street, Surry Hills, NSW 2010, Australia
enquiries@currency.com.au
www.currency.com.au

Typeset by Brighton Gray for Currency Press.
Printed by Fineline Print + Copy Services, Revesby, NSW.
Cover photography by Sare Clarke. Cover design by Katherine Zhang for Currency Press.

Currency Press acknowledges the Traditional Owners of the Country on which we live and work. We pay our respects to all Aboriginal and Torres Strait Islander Elders, past and present.

A catalogue record for this book is available from the National Library of Australia

Contents

Megan O'Connell as Angelica/Anna and Madeline Li as Elsa/Estée in New Ghosts Theatre Company's production of FRAME NARRATIVE *at The Old Fitz Theatre* (Photo: Phil Erbacher)

Madeline Li as Elsa/Estée and Charles Upton as Henrick/Hugh in New Ghosts Theatre Company's production of FRAME NARRATIVE *at The Old Fitz Theatre* (Photo: Phil Erbacher)

Co-parenting a play: on creating *Frame Narrative*

My first response to being asked to write this foreword was joy.

Of course, once the task arrived, joy quickly gave way to dread. For the past week, I've been grappling with how to articulate what this play means to me—how it has come to reflect so many facets of my life that were in flux during its making. I was in the twilight of my twenties, uncertain about relationships, navigating questions around motherhood and career, and staring down the start of a new job that looked a lot like shoes twelve sizes too big.

Add to that the challenge of articulating my deep gratitude to Emily, who trusted me to join her in co-parenting this work into existence, and to all the artists who made that possible.

So, here I go.

It's the 28th of June, 2025—I'm now 31. Otherwise, not a huge amount of change to report: still an aspiring mum, still wearing those big shoes, although a little more comfortably, at least. The same themes still take up my daily inner-monologue that did then—about ambition, about risk, and about what it means to birth big ideas into the world.

Last night, I was helping our Executive Producer Emma Wright prepare for her panel at the National Play Summit. One of the questions was: *What does ambition look like in playwriting?* We got surprisingly stumped on it. Is it about scale—grand sets, large casts, technical wizardry—or, can you really have an ambitious text?

Emma looked at me and said, 'Well… it's *Frame Narrative.*'

And she's right.

They say you have to know the rules to break them. Emily's razor-sharp dramaturgical brain is a case in point for this. She doesn't just break rules in this work—she bends form, structure, and tone in thrilling, unexpected ways. She has the guts to pull the rug from under the audience not just once, but twice. She straddles genre and media forms. She constructs characters that shift and refract across timelines—and yet, the story holds. That's the magic. That's the ambition.

Or so I thought.

On 1st of December, 2022, I sat down and read Draft 0 of *Frame Narrative* for the first time. I remember the experience viscerally, because it spoke so specifically to those themes of my life. Moments of the final act—depicting two creators debating authorship and collaboration within the four walls of their own theatre—could have been verbatim from my life. The work's deeply personal roots extended beyond Emily and found their way into my core too, reflecting where we both were at that moment in time: as women, as artists, as aspiring mothers.

But would anyone else feel the same way? Or had I just tapped into a story that was all for me and Emily, and for no one else?

Finally, I plucked up the courage to share it with Emma. She approached it with some skepticism—'what is this play that Lucy's been going on about for so long'—but after one read, she matched my unbridled excitement. The three of us formed a consortia, and began a journey together to bring *Frame Narrative* to the stage.

Much like raising a child, it takes a village to debut a new play, so our first task was to build out our creative team. Twenty-four theatre makers came together, from designers and managers to assistants and performers. As indie theatre, what our production lacked in money, we needed to make up for ten-fold in passion. As I watched our team cover their mouths during the first read—in that specific visceral shock that we reserve only for experiences that hit very close to home—I knew we had that ingredient down pat.

But, even as I saw more and more people responding just as I had on that December day, my doubt in *Frame Narrative*'s broader reception was still not completely quelled. Yes, this story spoke to all of us, as a women-led creative team. Problem was, 'female artist' is still a pretty niche audience. What about the rest of the community?

The great blessing and curse of theatre is that it can't exist without an audience. We waited in anticipation for that day to come, and for my doubts to finally be tested in a trial by fire. By this point, I'd spent sixteen months with this text. I could mouth along as the actors spoke it and was probably equipped (except for a lack of acting talent) to understudy all of them. But, like carrying a child to term before finally getting to meet it, I would learn so much more about *Frame Narrative* once it was out there interacting with the world.

Yes, the play was dramaturgically brilliant. Yes, it resonated with me and my specific circumstances. But what the audience taught me was that it wasn't just a story about artists. It's a much greater love letter to all those who create—to those who bring something into the world that didn't exist before, whether that be a story, a company, an idea, a child. Especially to those who dare to attempt more than one of those things in a single lifetime. Art versus artist, legacy versus presence, autobiography vs invention—these are not theoretical dichotomies. And when the person at the centre of those questions is a woman, the scale of the provocation multiplies. While these ideas felt so intimate, they were also epic—so much bigger than me, Emily, Emma, our industry, or even our community in Sydney or Australia. Beneath all the metatheatrics lies something undeniably human, universal, timeless.

My mind wanders forward to June 2025— just a week ago, when I had a conversation over drinks with a group of male friends. I casually asked, 'If your partner wanted your first-born child to take her last name, how would you feel?'

The answer came quickly: 'Not good. '

'And if she said this on a first date? '

'There wouldn't be a second.'

I had two thoughts in response to this. The first was that I should stop asking this on first dates. And the second was surprise at how radical this simple idea was, even in 2025 metropolitan Sydney. In a world where we're still fighting such large battles—lack of safety, financial inequality, discrimination—we rarely feel the space to turn the lens from macro to micro, and explore ideas that are closer to home, or everyday in nature. It's within this space, festering far further down the iceberg, that our *Frame Narrative* exists, simmering with guilt, frustration, contradiction, and vulnerability.

Emily confronts the contradictions between autobiography, authorship, aging and ambition—not as problems to solve, but as provocations to sit with. And in the true spirit of a frame narrative, these ideas even follow Emily into the process of the writing and creation of the work itself, which was both so inventive and personal. No matter how far you search, she doesn't present you with any answers. The play's very title nods to this structure—a story within a story—which it boldly embodies.

And that, to me, is what makes this play truly ambitious.

When Emma and I stepped into our new roles at the Old Fitz Theatre, we felt the weight of expectation. As a wonderful character in this play would so eloquently put it, our work could no longer just 'be'. It had to 'be good'. And it was up to Emily, Emma and I to achieve that. Thinking back—what a pressure-cooker situation we put ourselves in to get it there. All three of us sleeping under one roof during the rehearsal process—Emma and I in one room, Emily in the next. Emma not only producing the show, but also debuting the role of that aforementioned 'Playwright' character. Inspired by Emily? We weren't sure. But we sat at our breakfast table each morning, watching Emily's every move for inspiration, just in case. Emily, on the other hand, was not only getting ready for the birth of her play, but also the birth of her first child—which she carried as her own, personal secret. As Emma investigated and took on the shape of the heavily pregnant Playwright, Emily hid her own growing baby bump from the world. My own seed of doubt wasn't a secret, however, and we all talked about it late into the nights, wondering what everyone would think of this creation of ours.

Despite all that pressure, we never did become the Playwright and the Director of *Frame Narrative*'s Act 3, locked in creative combat or tearing each other apart. Instead, Emily, Emma and I stayed united through to the finish line. We remained a single team, in awe of our ensemble, and full of pride—not just for the work, but for each other. We all sat together one last time in the moments before Opening Night, and spoke about how the audience response no longer mattered to us. What had become most important wasn't how the work would be received, but the extraordinary process of making it—of building something together. That moment of connection, of collective risk-taking, was more meaningful than any review or accolade. I've rarely had an experience in this industry as rewarding.

And while the act of theatre is, by nature, fleeting—sets packed down, lights reset, scripts stored away—the relationships we forged through *Frame Narrative* remain. That is its legacy too: not just the play, but the village that made it.

I'm writing these final words from inside the Old Fitz, where transience claims centre stage. Last night a show closed, and this evening a new one bumps in. For a fleeting moment, the walls are black, the scaffolds bare, and the floor is empty. A liminal space. A shell in which so many stories have come before, reset and waiting for the next one.

Sixteen months it took to get *Frame Narrative* on the stage—and now, I write this exactly sixteen months since its set filled this space and told Emily's story. It feels like a lifetime ago, with 37 other stories having come and gone since. I'm reminded yet again of the idea that *Frame Narrative* gently puts forward—that maybe… maybe the art we create is greater than its creators. That feels true now. This play no longer belongs just to Emily, or me, or our team, or even to our audiences. It earns a place in the contemporary canon, demanding future life on stages yet unseen.

And now it will live on.

I'm deeply thankful to Currency Press for bringing this work into print. Now this story can reach new stages, new generations. It won't fade with memory or age, even if we do. It will continue to mirror the creatives who have the courage to bring it to life, grappling with their own ideas of authorship and collaboration. In mirroring its creators, *Frame Narrative* will change with the village that raises it: different audiences of artists, mothers, entrepreneurs, authors, creators, and women—who will be dared to think bigger, to challenge gendered expectations, and embrace all the messy contradiction, vulnerability and courage that comes with that. What a gift.

And to our beautiful Aoife Nieve Sheehan: Aren't you lucky to be named after your extraordinary mother? May you inherit her wisdom, her insight, her heart—and yes, her ambition.

This story belongs to you.

Lucy Clements

Artistic & Managing Director, Old Fitz Theatre

Madeline Li as Elsa/Estée in New Ghosts Theatre Company's production of FRAME NARRATIVE *2024 at The Old Fitz Theatre (Photo: Phil Erbacher)*

Charles Upton as The Director and Emma Wright as The Playwright in New Ghosts Theatre Company's production of FRAME NARRATIVE *at The Old Fitz Theatre (Photo: Phil Erbacher)*

Playwright's Note

Before my daughter was conceived, I kept thinking, *how will I do both?*

I feared the loss of self, the loss of time, but most of all, the loss of ambition. I feared boredom. I feared missing out. I also feared how much I would love her. Not because I didn't want that, but because I knew she would rearrange me. And I wasn't sure what would remain.

Then I was pregnant. And with her growing inside me, the fear went quiet—without me doing anything.

She's born, and I love her—wildly, without end. The love takes hold. It pulls like gravity. Rushes like blood. Somehow my body made this person. I look at her and think: *I made you. And you made me.*

The panic never arrived. The dread didn't show up. Instead, my world steadied. And I feel deeply, inexplicably still me.

Which is not to say my life was unchanged. It was. But I wasn't lost. I'm amazed at how motherhood has transformed every moment of my life, and yet I still feel completely myself in it.

The stories still call to me. The words line up in my mind. And when I sit down to write, I don't feel like a depleted version of who I was. I feel like the same artist, with new access points.

What I hadn't expected was that motherhood wouldn't crowd out my artistic self. It would intensify it. Sharpen it. Now, it's more direct. More honest. I get to the truth faster.

And the truth is this: I love being a mother.

There's a clarity I didn't have before: a visceral understanding of stakes, a sense that time is precious and risk is worth it.

Of course, the shape of my process has changed. But the impulse to write hasn't.

I don't write because I'm scared of losing something. I write because I want to continue to know myself. To trace my thinking, my heart, the way I feel about the world. I hope she will one day recognise me in my words.

The fear was never in the baby. It was of the unknown. And now, I know her.

* * *

I started writing *Frame Narrative* about a year before my partner and I would entertain the idea of starting a family. It's a messy puzzle of a play and it takes me a long time to work through the ideas.

I work on the second draft while on a writing placement in Scotland, and then England. I'm thinking about storytelling, the gothic, and authorial mythology. I keep returning to feminine authorship—how men are allowed to explore 'big ideas' while women are assumed to be mining their personal lives. I'm struck by how the classics are treated as important and universal, while new work—especially new Australian work—is considered niche. Personal. Small. (Personal always means small.) I feel rage as I write my way through the play's central dramatic questions.

Quietly, I'm also thinking about motherhood—not urgently, but it's there. When I return home to Australia, the plan is to begin trying for a baby. In some ways, you might say there was a deadline. Although I don't think of it that way now.

I arrive home in Melbourne in August. That month, my friend Lucy Clements tells me she will soon be the new Artistic Director of The Old Fitz Theatre. It's not yet announced. But she wants to direct *Frame Narrative* as her first show in her inaugural season in March. Rehearsals will begin in January. Four months from now. My partner and I haven't started trying. But I know—quietly, secretly—that if I say yes, there is a real possibility I will be pregnant during the process. And the play is not yet finished.

I do the math in my head: *if we conceive this month…*

Until this point, my life was informing the art. But now, it felt like the art was spilling over into my life.

I tell Lucy I don't know if I can finish the play in time. I've been circling the same dramatic questions for months. The story keeps folding in on itself and rewriting its meaning as it goes. I know what it wants to be, but I don't know how to make it hold. And now, with this timeline—and this quiet possibility of imminent motherhood—it feels even more precarious.

Lucy is calm. She says she trusts me. She says it will come together.

And I do believe her. But I can't shake the feeling that I'm writing toward something I haven't resolved in myself. The play is asking questions I don't have answers to.

I say yes to the production. And the following month, I'm pregnant. I take a pregnancy test in the early hours of the morning before a flight to Sydney. We're squeezing in a script development workshop before Christmas. I meet with a writing agent I'm trying to woo. I finish the draft over the Christmas break. By rehearsals, I'm twelve weeks. No one knows. I feel porous. The play is becoming real. So is the baby.

In the room, Lucy is a force. Steady, incisive, unafraid of complexity. She makes space for discovery, for risk. The play's focus is sharpening and I rewrite to keep up with our discoveries. My body is changing. My world is changing. But in the room, I'm the playwright.

Under Lucy's direction, the production comes together with precision. It takes a village to bring new plays to the stage. And Lucy, alongside our sensational producer Emma Wright, steers a mammoth team of twenty-four artists towards opening night. It's a truly incredible feat for independent theatre.

* * *

I think about what a frame narrative is—a story within a story. How the outer story shapes the inner one. And the inner story, once understood, reframes everything we thought we knew about the outer. That's what motherhood feels like to me. She's not the whole story. But she changes the way I read the rest of it.

* * *

The play closes. And my girl, Aoife, is born some months later. Time passes. I reread the script to get it ready for publication. I avoid this task for some time. I thought I would cringe at parts of it. Want to rewrite it with everything I know now. But I don't. I'm surprised by how it still feels deeply true.

I wish I could tell my past self that writing doesn't have to come after understanding. Sometimes it comes before, even alongside it, and helps to make sense of what follows.

* * *

What I feared might happen, did: I love her more than anything I could ever write.

And still, I write. With the biggest love I've ever known asleep in the next room.

Emily Sheehan, May 2025

Acknowledgements

My heartfelt thank you to the artists who helped me write this play. Particularly Lucy Clements, who directed its premiere season at The Old Fitz Theatre and Tamar Saphra, my dramaturg, who so precisely guided the play's emotional throughline. Thank you also to our producer Emma Wright, our five brilliant actors, and the beautiful design team, for building the world, sharing your insights, and for the joy you brought to solving this puzzle together.

For Aoife.
Who wasn't there in the beginning
but arrived in the messy middle
and gave the end its meaning.
You are my best creation.

Megan O'Connell as Angelica/Anna in New Ghosts Theatre Company's production of FRAME NARRATIVE *at The Old Fitz Theatre (Photo: Phil Erbacher)*

Frame Narrative was first produced by New Ghosts Theatre Company and performed at The Old Fitz Theatre on March 8, 2024 with the following cast:

ANGELICA / ANNA / ACTOR 1	Megan O'Connell
ELSA / ESTÉE / ACTOR 2	Madeline Li
HENRICK / HUGH / THE DIRECTOR	Charles Upton
MARGOT / ACTOR 3	Jennifer Rani
THE PLAYWRIGHT	Emma Wright

Director, Lucy Clements
Producer, Emma Wright
Set Designer, Soham Apte
Costume Designer, Rita Naidu
Sound Designer, Sam Cheng
Lighting Designer, Spencer Herd
Dramaturg, Tamar Saphra
Stage Manager, Alex Liang
Assistant Stage Manager, Oscar Ali
Intimacy Coordinator, Shondelle Pratt
Assistant Director, Jeremi Campese
Assistant Set & Costume Designer, Bella Wellstead
Assistant Sound Designer, Sparks Sanders Robinson
Assistant Lighting Designer, Isobel Morrissey

CHARACTERS

This play is written in three parts, for five actors. In each part they become an altered version of their previous character. These transformations are:

ANGELICA / ANNA / ACTOR 1
ELSA / ESTÉE / ACTOR 2
HENRICK / HUGH / THE DIRECTOR
MARGOT / ACTOR 3
THE PLAYWRIGHT

In Part Two we also hear the voices of a film crew: FIRST AD, SOUND, DP, 2ND AC, CLAPPER, MEDIC. These roles could be seen or unseen, depending on the scale of the production.

LOCATION

Similarly, the location remains the same but its context transforms. These shifts are:

Part One: A chalet in the Swiss Alps.

Part Two: A film shoot 'on location' in a chalet in the Swiss Alps.

Part Three: A theatre stage representing a film shoot on location in the Swiss Alps.

A NOTE ON STYLE

Similarly, the tone and style of the play should have a clear and distinct shift in each part. How this is realised is open to interpretation. Some initial provocations:

Part One: Gothic, moody, 'European'.

Part Two: Psychological, horror, 'American'.

Part Three: Naturalistic, self conscious, 'Australian'.

PART ONE

SCENE ONE

A chalet in the Swiss Alps at the base of Mont Blanc, about an hour by train from Geneva.

THE PLAYWRIGHT *writes by the light of a desk lamp. She moves between typing on a laptop and scribbling in her notebook.*

Mounted to the wall above her is a vintage pistol.

Then lightning strikes! And suddenly THE PLAYWRIGHT *is replaced by* ANGELICA THORNE *(forties), a revered film director.* ANGELICA *does the same pattern of activity as* THE PLAYWRIGHT*: moving between typing on a laptop and scribbling in her notebook.*

A loud buzz from the intercom gives ANGELICA *a fright.*

She pulls herself out of her mountain of notebooks and goes to the intercom.

She buzzes the visitor in.

After a moment, ELSA MÜLLER *(twenties) enters through the door, dressed stylishly though inexpensively. She holds a posy of lavender wrapped in brown paper. A leather satchel is slung over her shoulder.*

ANGELICA *and* ELSA*'s accents reflect they are in Switzerland, but they could be from anywhere in Europe.*

ANGELICA: You're late.

ELSA: I know, the train—

ANGELICA: You were scheduled for four thirty.

ELSA: It's four thirty-seven.

ANGELICA: I've wrapped for the day.

ELSA: Don't I have until five?

ANGELICA: I've been doing press since seven this morning. Talking talking talking. I can't face another minute.

ELSA: [*offering the flowers*] These are for you.

ANGELICA: …

ELSA: From my editor. I'll put them in water?
ANGELICA: On the table's fine.
ELSA: Congratulations on the film.
ANGELICA: Thank you.
ELSA: They're saying she's tipped for best actress at Cannes.
ANGELICA: Mmmm.
ELSA: She has an unhinged quality to her performance.
ANGELICA: She's exquisite.
ELSA: What was the casting process like?
ANGELICA: No. No. We're not doing that.
ELSA: Doing what?
ANGELICA: Sorry, kid.
ELSA: [*extending her hand*] Elsa Müller.
ANGELICA: Is that a pen name?
ELSA: I've seen all your films.
ANGELICA: You and every other wide-eyed critic today.
ELSA: Multiple times. But more than that: I get you.
ANGELICA: You 'get me'?
ELSA: This film in particular; I felt a deep affinity with.
ANGELICA: You know the last train back to Geneva is at six.
ELSA: I'll make it.
ANGELICA: If you're quick you might pick up a ride down the mountain, back to the station.
ELSA: I can walk.
ANGELICA: Did you see the forecast?
ELSA: No?
ANGELICA: There's a storm on its way.
ELSA: I only need fifteen minutes of your time.
ANGELICA: I have dinner reservations. My guest will be arriving.
ELSA: I'll be gone by five p.m.

A suspended pause; neither will relent.

ANGELICA: Where are you from?
ELSA: *Paradis Perdu*.
ANGELICA: Never heard of it.
ELSA: We're an independent publication.
ANGELICA: Most outlets do this by telephone.

ELSA: It had to be in person.

ANGELICA: You're not a horrible tabloid are you?

ELSA: A quarterly print journal. We publish non-fiction, flash fiction, essays, social commentary, arts criticism, photojournalism and poetry.

ANGELICA *assesses her.*

ANGELICA: What's your angle?

ELSA: I'm writing a longform essay on your past, your lived experiences, how they echo across your body of work.

ANGELICA: [*sarcastically*] How original.

ELSA: I want the backstory that explains why your films are so dark and honest.

Pause.

I'm a big fan.

Pause.

Please? I fought hard for this gig.

ANGELICA: And you blew it.

ELSA *nods. She rests the bouquet on the table.*

ELSA: Well, then … Au revoir. (Goodbye.) For what it's worth, I do love your work. I've watched your talks. I've read your essays. It's an honour to have met you, Ms Thorne.

Just before ELSA *exits,* ANGELICA *relents.*

ANGELICA: [*annoyed with herself for surrendering*] Sit down.

ELSA: Merci! (Thank you!)

ANGELICA: You have fifteen minutes.

ELSA: C'est bon, c'est bon. (That's fine, that's fine.)

ANGELICA: But I need a drink in my hand. There's a bottle somewhere.

ANGELICA *rummages through the pile of media gifts to find a bottle of whiskey.*

ELSA *delights in details of the chalet. She spies the vintage gun on display.*

ELSA: Nice pistol.

ANGELICA *smiles.*

ELSA: Is that the original? From the film—?

ANGELICA: It is.

ELSA: I can't believe I'm standing in the house. *In this very room.*

ANGELICA: It's marvellous, isn't it?

ELSA: And this is where she gets her revenge?

ANGELICA: Yes.

ELSA: On this lounge right here? She takes the pistol—

ANGELICA: That set piece was tricky.

ELSA: Raises it to him—

ANGELICA: We might have done around eighty takes before getting it right.

ELSA: And boom!

Beat.

I'm curious to know: are those scenes from your early films real? Did you do all those things?

ANGELICA: Why would that matter?

ELSA: I don't know how you'd come up with some of that stuff if it hadn't happened to you.

ANGELICA *smiles, maybe half-acknowledges, but doesn't give an answer.*

I suppose you're an artist. That's what you do. Come up with crazy, wild stories.

ANGELICA: Some of it's imagined, some of it's from conversations with friends, and some of it is real.

ANGELICA *finishes pouring herself a whiskey. She takes a sip.*

ANGELICA: That's two minutes.

ELSA *takes a notebook from her satchel. She flicks furiously to find the page.*

ELSA: First question: why an adaptation? Why this departure for you?

ANGELICA: Why not?

ELSA: But why now? Why not something original?

ANGELICA: There was a point, early on, where I made very diaristic work. But these days? My world feels more open creatively.

ELSA: Second question. This line, in the film, is the only direct quote from the original text:

ELSA *reads aloud from her notebook. She quotes from Mary Shelley's* Frankenstein.

'Adam had come forth from the hands of God a perfect creature, happy and prosperous, guarded by the especial care of his Creator.'

ANGELICA: You've done your homework.

ELSA: 'I am thy creature; I ought to be thy Adam. Yet you, my Creator, detest and spurn me.' Why this passage?

ANGELICA: The Creature is envious of Adam and Eve. The originals. And their relationship with their maker. By comparison, the Creature is a pale imitation.

ELSA: But unlike most modern interpretations, your film's point of view resists sympathising with the Creature. Why?

ANGELICA: I don't like to be so heavy-handed.

ELSA: [*reading from her notes*] 'I am thy creature; you are my maker.'

ANGELICA: You feel for him?

ELSA: I do.

ANGELICA: We mustn't feel for, and over-psychologise, monstrous men.

ELSA: We're all our worst selves when we're rejected.

ANGELICA: We don't all go on a murder spree.

ELSA: But it's Victor's fault, don't you think? The original sin was his. Anything his Creature does, Victor has to take responsibility.

ANGELICA: Playing God is hardly a sin by today's standards.

ELSA: When Victor is creating the Creature—when he is pregnant with the idea—he is full of excitement and anticipation. But once it's born, he hates it. And he hates himself for creating it.

ANGELICA: Must we love everything we create?

ELSA: Don't you?

ANGELICA: [*shrugging*] Hmph.

ELSA: Then why make it?

ANGELICA: Why does anyone make anything? The driving force is God-like. But the results we cannot control.

ELSA: Are you happy with the results?

ANGELICA: It's not what I imagined, but it's an interesting attempt at something.

ELSA: An attempt to reveal something about yourself, perhaps?

ANGELICA: Perhaps.

ELSA: A secret?

ANGELICA: A different part of me. A part that's been … [*Correcting*] An aesthetic I haven't had access to. [*Switching*] But like I said, that doesn't mean I control or even like the results.

ELSA: *Well, I like your films.* I'm a big fan. I've watched them over and over. I deconstruct your stories. Pour over the minutia. It makes me feel part of the narrative.

ANGELICA: Well, that's … I'm glad you feel something for the art.

ELSA: *For you.*

ANGELICA: I'm just the vessel.

ELSA: You're the maker.

Beat.

Do you see yourself in Victor?

ANGELICA: Not particularly.

ELSA: You don't long to create life?

ANGELICA *gives her a look, like, 'Really?'*

I just mean to say the passages you quote, the visual motifs: they're about motherhood, aren't they?

ANGELICA: I get into the mindset of all of my characters. Even for an adaptation. I still have to find a point of entry: my own empathy or parallels.

ELSA: But something's changed in your work. Your films used to be about sex.

She flicks through her notes.

But now, they're about mother nature, maternal yearning. You're obsessed with it.

ANGELICA: [*making a 'no' sound*] Mmmm.

ELSA: You don't think so?

ANGELICA: You're trying to see something that isn't there.

ELSA: What am I trying to see?

ANGELICA: I'm not doing that.

ELSA: Doing what?

ANGELICA: Audiences always project aspects of themselves onto a story. It's part of the artistic exchange. A good storyteller will allow space for it.

ELSA: You're saying I'm the one projecting these things?

ANGELICA: Maybe. Are you riddled with 'maternal yearning'?

ELSA: *You can't deny your work has changed.*

ANGELICA: Perhaps it's you who's changed. And now different aspects speak to you.

ELSA: So the film wasn't art imitating life?

ANGELICA: No, it's art imitating itself.

ELSA: I think you're lying.

ANGELICA: That's very narrow-minded of you, you know? 'Men write about ideas. Women write about their personal life.' I've heard it all before.

ELSA: But you've hidden secret messages across your whole body of work. In the background of shots, the lyrics in the soundtracks, the costume choices.

ANGELICA: [*dismissive*] *Mmmm, secret messages.*

ELSA: In your first film, the young ingénue, who is well-known to be based on you, wears a small, gold, fig leaf pendant. In this film, Victor wears the same necklace.

ANGELICA: You have done your homework.

ELSA: [*connecting the dots*] Fig leaves. Adam and Eve. Garden of Eden. *Paradise Lost. Frankenstein.* Everything tumbles into itself.

ANGELICA: Art imitating art.

ELSA: Mise-en-abyme.

ANGELICA: A picture within a picture.

ELSA: I believe you are still making films about your life, but in a veiled way.

ANGELICA: This one is fiction. It's more than fiction—it's an adaptation. It's not even original.

ELSA: [*realising*] Oh gosh! It's so clever that your most personal work yet could be an adaptation.

ANGELICA: …

ELSA: What you're pouring into it: ambition, the drive to create. Joy and anticipation followed by the true horror of regret. It's confessional.

ANGELICA: And what am I confessing?

ELSA: …

ANGELICA: Go on.

ELSA: There are rumours you had a child.

ANGELICA: …

ELSA: In your youth. You gave birth to a child who died.

ANGELICA: I've never heard those rumours.

ELSA: They're out there.

ANGELICA: Whatever rumours you've heard, I haven't heard them. Which means they're baseless enough to not even work their way back to me.

ELSA: They're all variations on the same.

ANGELICA: Is this going to be in your essay?

ELSA: Born in London and raised single-handedly by your father, a radical philosopher. At sixteen, you fall in love with a married poet, and together you run off to France. You fall pregnant almost immediately. The poet is still married. Your father is furious. After spending a summer gallivanting across Europe, you run out of money. You grow more and more pregnant. You keep changing addresses to avoid debt collectors. The poet learns his wife has committed suicide. Her lifeless body is discovered in the Serpentine.

Beat.

You give birth. Prematurely. A little girl.

ANGELICA *begins laughing.*

You name her Clara. She dies just days after birth. Years later, she becomes the subject of your masterpiece. Sorry—you're laughing?

ANGELICA: It's funny!

ELSA: Are you nervous?

ANGELICA: It's so predictable. *Rumours about a child?*

ELSA: I know these are personal questions. It must be quite emotional to have to clarify these things.

ANGELICA: A successful, talented, woman makes films that deal with real world themes, like sex and creation, and we project onto it. *That must be her life. Those must be her traumas.* There must be a harrowing backstory that explains why it feels so true.

ELSA: What's the cost of admitting it? Off the record.

ANGELICA: I think that's our time.

ELSA: So you deny the child's existence or you decline to comment?

ANGELICA: Why don't you take your notebook and your flowers and get the hell out of my house.

The lights flicker.

ELSA: What was that?

ANGELICA: The electrics. Happens in these old houses.

The lights flicker again. ELSA *startles.*

The storm. I warned you. Good luck getting down the mountain now.

ELSA: … I'll get going then.

ELSA *goes to leave, then fawns.*

I'm sorry. I honestly love your work so much, I let my imagination run with the idea.

ANGELICA: Well, it's nonsense, so …

ELSA: None of it will be in my essay.

ANGELICA: Look, I can give you some quotes for the piece, but you must promise not to mix fact and fiction.

ELSA *nods.*

Who do you write for again?

ELSA: *Paradis Perdu.* (*Paradise Lost.*)

ANGELICA: Who's the editor there?

ELSA: John Milton.

It's familiar, but she can't place it.

ANGELICA: John Milton. Huh.

ELSA: He's going to be so angry with me.

ANGELICA: Well, he doesn't have to know. If none of it's in your essay, he won't have to call me for comment, and I won't have to recount to him … Wait, John who?

ELSA: Milton. *Paradis Perdu*— [*Translating*] *Paradise Lost.*

Then she knows.

ANGELICA: Who are you? Why are you in my home?

ELSA: Come on. *You know who I am, Angelica.*

ANGELICA: No, I don't.

ELSA: If you had to guess.

ANGELICA: I have no idea.

ELSA: You're being coy now?

ANGELICA: You need to tell me who you are, or I'll call the police.

ELSA: It should be obvious.
ANGELICA: Fine, the police can tell me who you are.
ELSA: It's me. It's Clara.

The rain begins.

ANGELICA: Did somebody put you up to this?
ELSA: You didn't answer my letters.
ANGELICA: I didn't get any letters. I'm not who you think I am.
ELSA: I had to meet you.
ANGELICA: You need to leave. I'll call you a taxi.
ELSA: No. Please, Maman. (Please, Mother.)
ANGELICA: Don't call me that.
ELSA: I've longed for this moment.
ANGELICA: Listen, Elsa.
ELSA: Clara.
ANGELICA: Elsa, I've had your type before.
ELSA: It's the truth.
ANGELICA: You're not the first journalist to make up stories like this.
ELSA: I can prove it.

The storm swells. The lights trip, leaving them in darkness.

ANGELICA: [*in darkness*] The lights! … Where are you?

The lights flicker, revealing ELSA *in a different part of the room.* ANGELICA *startles.*

The storm creeps into the language.

Asterisks now mark text from Mary Shelley's Frankenstein.

ANGELICA *gasps, startled.*

ELSA: You deny me?*
ANGELICA: Stay away from me.
ELSA: Don't be afraid.*
ANGELICA: What do you want?!
ELSA: I expected this reception.*

The lights trip again.

The lights flick on, revealing ELSA *now very close to* ANGELICA.

I am thy creature. I ought to be thy Adam.*
ANGELICA: We are strangers.*

ELSA: You, my Creator, detest and spurn me?*
ANGELICA: There can be no relationship between you and me.*
ELSA: You are my maker.*

Thunder.

A loud BUZZ from the intercom gives them both a fright. They jump back from each other. What just happened between them?

After a moment, more buzzes from the intercom.

HENRICK: [*over the intercom*] Allo?
ANGELICA: That will be my dinner date.
HENRICK: [*over the intercom*] It's Henrick.
ELSA: Henrick? Not the famous actor Henrick Bergman?
ANGELICA: …
ELSA: From your films?!
ANGELICA: … Yes.
HENRICK: [*over the intercom*] Angelica? Can you buzz me in?
ELSA: … Well don't keep him waiting.

ANGELICA *hesitates but decides to let him in.*

ANGELICA: [*into the intercom*] It's open.

She buzzes him in. They wait.

After a moment, the door opens. HENRICK BERGMAN *(thirties), a very 'serious' actor, arrives, soaked from the rain.*

HENRICK: I'm soaked.
ELSA: [*speaking Swiss-French*] Bonsoir! (Good evening!)
HENRICK: My shoes are soaked through. I'll get mud everywhere. Can you get me something to stand on?

ANGELICA *finds him a newspaper.*

ELSA: Mademoiselle Müller. It's a pleasure to meet you.
HENRICK: [*speaking German*] Guten abend. (Good evening.) [*To* ANGELICA] You have company?
ANGELICA: She's part of the press. She's writing a piece on me.
ELSA: Congratulations on the film.
HENRICK: Did you like it?
ELSA: Yes, yes! I have so many questions.
ANGELICA: We were just wrapping up.

ELSA: I still have some questions on my list, if you don't mind?

ANGELICA: Henrick Bergman is a very busy man. I'm sure you understand.

ELSA: You said you'd introduce us.

A tense pause.

HENRICK: Everything okay?

ANGELICA: Of course. Where are my manners? This is my long term collaborator, Monsieur Henrick Bergman. Leading man. Heartthrob of Europe. Henrick; Mademoiselle Müller.

ELSA: Call me Clara.

ANGELICA: She's a young writer. Very ambitious. Very creative. We're lucky to have her writing an essay about—

ELSA: About her past.

ANGELICA: About how my past work informs what I make today.

HENRICK: Well, happy writing, Mademoiselle. Your subject is certainly exquisite.

ELSA: You're such intimate collaborators. I'm sure you have some insights?

HENRICK: I have a few stories …

ELSA: I want the truth that explains why her films are so dark and honest.

HENRICK: Well, *how long do you have?*

HENRICK *and* ELSA *laugh,* ANGELICA *doesn't.*

ANGELICA: Well, we have dinner reservations, so—

HENRICK: Not until seven.

ANGELICA: *With the storm, Henrick,* we should head off.

HENRICK: Come now, I can answer one question.

ANGELICA: Taxis will be hard to come by in this rain.

HENRICK: [*to* ELSA] So long as you give us a good write-up, huh? Front cover.

ANGELICA: [*flirtatious, cautious*] Henrick, don't say anything you don't want quoted.

HENRICK: On the record: *she's mad!* Completely insane.

ANGELICA: He's being silly.

HENRICK: Writes for hours and hours and hours into the night. So tortured. So self-punishing.

ANGELICA: All lies.

HENRICK: Engaged, heart and soul, in one pursuit. Exploring the deepest mysteries of creation.

ANGELICA: He's like this. He likes to make up stories.

HENRICK: Come now, Angelica. Let me play into a few artistic cliches for our friend here.

ELSA: What do you mean?

HENRICK: I mean, it's a matter of perception, isn't it? When you're asking people to invest in the idea of a genius, well, people need to see the tortured artist.

ELSA: And if she's a tortured artist, what do you think tortures her?

HENRICK: Well … you'll have to watch the film to find out.

Thunder. The rain picks up.

Ha! There's your quote. And with that, I'm done.

ANGELICA: You'll be off now, I suppose?

ELSA: There's still so much to talk about.

HENRICK: Be careful on the road, it gets slippery down the mountain.

ELSA: I said, there's still so much we have to talk about.

ANGELICA: … Why don't you come back tomorrow? We can talk then.

ELSA: Tomorrow?

ANGELICA: For as long as you like.

ELSA: …

ANGELICA: You'd be smart to get to the station before the storm hits.

ELSA: I don't think I'll make the last train.

ANGELICA: You will if you leave now.

ELSA: Is it safe to walk down the mountain?

ANGELICA: Take his bicycle.

ELSA: I couldn't possibly.

ANGELICA: Take his bicycle. Leave it at the station. We'll send someone for it tomorrow.

HENRICK: The keys to the bike lock are hidden in the electrical box.

ELSA: Keys in the electrical box. Got it.

ELSA *collects her satchel.*

Enjoy your night.

ELSA *departs quickly, the door slamming behind her.*

ANGELICA *sighs in relief. She makes her way to the window and peers through the curtains to check* ELSA*'s left.*

ANGELICA: Henrick, if she returns, you mustn't let her in.
HENRICK: I'll call us a taxi for dinner.
ANGELICA: Promise me.
HENRICK: You're worried about that girl?
ANGELICA: We need to call the police.
HENRICK: Who is she?
ANGELICA: A nasty little stalker. She's obsessed with me.
HENRICK: The price of fame, huh? I'll call a taxi.

ANGELICA *spies the pistol. She moves towards the gun and takes it off its display. Holding it in her hands.*

Angelica? Hello?
ANGELICA: …
HENRICK: Put that thing back.
ANGELICA: It's vintage; it's defective.
HENRICK: Come. Sit with me.

ANGELICA *goes back to look out the window, taking the gun with her.*

ANGELICA: [*looking out the window*] Huh. The moon.*
HENRICK: Come away from the window.
ANGELICA: She's reached her summit in the heavens and is beginning to descend.*
HENRICK: Why are you acting strange?
ANGELICA: That girl.
HENRICK: What are you afraid of?
ANGELICA: An intruder.
HENRICK: What might an intruder do?
ANGELICA: Horrible things.
HENRICK: Here, let me take your mind off it.
ANGELICA: I can't be distracted from this.*

He gently takes the pistol from her and places it back on the display.

HENRICK: Okay. Then let's say there was an intruder outside that door. But let's imagine he's— [*Describing himself now*] {tall, olive skin, dark curls in his hair.} Very handsome. Very well dressed.

ANGELICA: … Okay.

HENRICK: And you're just his type.

ANGELICA: What's his type?

HENRICK: Beautiful. Rich. Fucking crazy.

ANGELICA: How does he know that?

HENRICK: He's seen your films.

She smiles. Welcoming the distraction.

ANGELICA: He's a fan.

HENRICK: He's become obsessed.

ANGELICA: He feels he knows me.

HENRICK: He starts sending letters.

ANGELICA: When he gets no reply, he begins digging. He discovers there's a home I retreat to during summer. A chalet in the Swiss Alps, about an hour by train from Geneva, at the base of Mont Blanc.

HENRICK: He takes the train journey to the small village and begins his search.

ANGELICA: He wanders the flea market, the flower stalls, the small church in the town square. The secondhand bookshop.

HENRICK: And then, one Sunday, he spies you in the delicatessen. He follows you in. Watches you order. Catches your pin code at the cashier when you're being sloppy. He remembers it.

ANGELICA: He tries the same pincode on the gate at the entrance. It works.

HENRICK: The storm covers the sound of the gates opening. He walks down the gravel driveway, approaching the house. He lets himself in.

ANGELICA: I'm in the shower.

HENRICK: He pours himself a whisky. From the good bottle. He knows the difference.

ANGELICA: I'm in the bathroom, but I hear the glass clink on the counter top.

HENRICK: You're afraid.

ANGELICA: No.

HENRICK: No?

ANGELICA: I'm thrilled! But, but, I can't let him know that.

HENRICK: No.

ANGELICA: I play dumb. I call out, 'Henrick, is that you?'
HENRICK: He knocks back the whiskey and readies himself.
ANGELICA: I come out in a silk nightgown.
HENRICK: You lock eyes.

HENRICK, *now in character as the intruder.* ANGELICA, *now in character as herself.*

'Enjoy your shower?'
ANGELICA: 'That's my whiskey.'
HENRICK: 'Look who's angry.'
ANGELICA: 'I don't like people helping themselves.'
HENRICK: Stay angry.
ANGELICA: How angry?
HENRICK: Rageful.
ANGELICA: She gets the pistol!
HENRICK: [*breaking, as* HENRICK] Ah-ah-ah—

ANGELICA *takes the vintage pistol from its display on the wall.*

ANGELICA: [*aiming it at him*] Yes! She sees it before he does and—
HENRICK: [*breaking, as* HENRICK] Put that thing down.
ANGELICA: It's defective, but he doesn't know that.
HENRICK: [*serious, as* HENRICK] No guns.
ANGELICA: Fine.

ANGELICA *places the gun down on her desk.*

She approaches him. Gets right up close. And spits. Full force. Into his face.
HENRICK: 'You want me to leave?' He enunciates.
ANGELICA: 'No. I want you to stay.'

A shadow in the doorway, and ELSA *appears inside the room, unnoticed by* ANGELICA *and* HENRICK.

'Tell me you're a monster.'
HENRICK: 'I'm a monster.'
ANGELICA: 'Will you harm me?'
HENRICK: 'If that's your desire.'
ANGELICA: 'I desire your darkness. Unleash it upon me!'
HENRICK: 'As you wish.'

The game is on. ELSA *watches, not realising it's a game.*

ANGELICA: 'I won't submit easily.'
HENRICK: He's excited now.
ANGELICA: 'Chase me then, you monster.'
HENRICK: 'You want a monster? I'll show you a monster.'

He moves in quickly, but she dodges.

ELSA *picks up the pistol.*

'Get back here.'
ANGELICA: 'Stay away from me!'
HENRICK: 'You can't run from me, Angelica.'
ANGELICA: She reaches the front door.

She tries the handle, feigning.

But it's locked!
HENRICK: He closes in.
ANGELICA: She's out of breath.
HENRICK: 'I have you cornered now.'
ANGELICA: 'What are you going to do to me?'
HENRICK: 'What I've been longing for.'
ANGELICA: 'Are you going to *kill me*?'
HENRICK: 'Yes. I'm going to kill you.'

ELSA *raises the pistol to shoot* HENRICK.

ELSA: STOP!

ANGELICA *and* HENRICK *turn around to discover* ELSA.

ANGELICA *screams.*

Then the ring of a sound-stage bell.

We hear the voice of a fourth person amplified.

MARGOT: [*'God voice' on mic*] And cut!

The gothic world dissolves and swirls into the next …

END OF PART ONE

PART TWO

SCENE TWO

We are now on a film shoot, on location in a chalet in the Swiss Alps. This world is distinctly 'American' and the gothic melodrama of Part One is now replaced by a more psychological tone.

ANGELICA THORNE *is now* ANNA, *the actor playing the role of* ANGELICA.

ELSA MÜLLER *is now* ESTÉE, *the actor playing the role of* ELSA.

HENRICK BERGMAN *is now* HUGH, *the actor playing the role of* HENRICK.

A fourth person enters the frame: MARGOT, *the film's director. Her clothing clashes with the others who are 'in costume'.* MARGOT *wears a puffer jacket, sneakers, a cap. Maybe she wears protective gear like headphones and safety goggles.*

MARGOT: [*'God voice' on mic*] Thank you everyone! That was great.

FIRST AD: [*'God voice' on mic*] Okay team, take lunch. We have one hour so all crew is to be back on set and ready to go by two-thirty to set up for Scene Four. Actors, you'll go straight into make-up. Please be mindful, there will be scaffolders working over the break, so no-one is to be on the set. And can we get the gun back in the gun safe, please?

MARGOT: Estée, can we get that back in the safe? And remember, angle *away from his face* when you're holding it.

ESTÉE *puts the pistol in the gun safe.*

ESTÉE: We're not doing actual blanks?

MARGOT: No, we're adding all that in post.

ESTÉE: But there's a box of blanks right here?

MARGOT: Blanks aren't safe. The gas is pressurised and shoots out extremely fast. So it's only harmless if you're handling it correctly.

The actors break for lunch. Depending on the staging, they may remain visible, milling around in puffer jackets, helping themselves to snacks from the catering table.

ANNA *doesn't join them.* MARGOT *approaches her.*

MARGOT: That take was great.

ANNA: Really?

MARGOT: You two are amazing together.

ANNA: …

MARGOT: Do you want to go eat?

ANNA: I'm going to need an empty stomach for the scene coming up.

MARGOT: You look great.

Pause.

Go on. Have a decent meal with everyone.

ANNA: [*trailing off*] My metabolism isn't …

MARGOT: I'm paying a fortune for catering.

ANNA: …

MARGOT: You want me to grab you something for later?

ANNA: It's fine. I need a quiet moment.

ANNA *goes to take her break,* MARGOT *calls her back:*

MARGOT: Estée's great, isn't she?

ANNA: Mmmm.

MARGOT: Powerful.

ANNA: Yeah.

MARGOT: You know she never trained?

ANNA: Mmmm.

MARGOT: She's not antiseptic like the rest of Hollywood. She's a big fan of yours.

ANNA: Really?

MARGOT: She was thrilled when we suggested you for casting.

ANNA: My work's a bit early for her to remember?

MARGOT: She said she wouldn't do it with anyone else.

ANNA: She said that?

MARGOT: Apparently nineties horror is doing the rounds on TikTok. It's like retro—

ANNA: Retro. Wow.

MARGOT: No, not retro. Ironic! That's the one. 'Ironic nostalgia'.

ANNA: Ironic?

MARGOT: Raunch culture, nineties trash—of which you were the quintessential scream queen—is all the rage.

ANNA: Well … I'll have to tell my agent that.

Pause.

MARGOT: That last take was great.

ANNA: You're the only director I'd do this for.

MARGOT: [*passing* ANNA *the sides*] So here's the new sides for tomorrow.

ANNA: [*taking them*] Great.

MARGOT: And the revised callsheet. Hope this doesn't mess with your prep.

ANNA: No, whatever you need.

MARGOT *goes to leave,* ANNA *calls out.*

[*Reading the schedule*] Oh!

MARGOT: Yes?

ANNA: These are all my … ?

MARGOT: What was that?

ANNA: These are all pickups on my work?

MARGOT: … *No.*

ANNA: Come on, Margot.

MARGOT: It's not like that.

ANNA: Margot, please. I said yes to this to work with you. So work with me.

MARGOT: Watching you through the camera, I can see you're holding onto something. You're protecting yourself.

ANNA: I'll work on that.

MARGOT: And tonally, you're still giving 'American nineties horror', you know? But this isn't that. This is more European.

ANNA: … I'll work on that.

MARGOT: Your work in *The House on the Cul de Sac*? When you're running down the street, barefoot, in your tiny silk teddy, *screaming*, just pushed right to the edge in fear for your life? *That's* the performance I'm after.

ANNA: Those roles were a blur of booze and cocaine.

MARGOT: [*shrugging to suggest, 'Well, why not'?*] *Well …*

ANNA: [*reassuring*] I'm sober now.

MARGOT: That's great.

Long pause.

ANNA: My return to cinema has to be, 'Wow!' You know?

MARGOT: Why don't the four of us have dinner after we wrap? We'll stay back. Order some food. We can discuss the new material.

ANNA *nods.*

MARGOT *joins the group.*

An extended quiet murmur, while various background bits and pieces happen around ANNA. *She watches the construction of it all.*

SCENE THREE

*The team—*MARGOT, ANNA, ESTÉE *and* HUGH*—eat dinner together around the set table. They have their scripts out next to their plates and have been discussing the material.*

They pass dishes back and forth throughout the scene, family-dinner style.

ANNA *sits at the head of the table. High status. Watching everyone.*

MARGOT: [*laughing*] And then! And then she just slapped him in the face!

ESTÉE: [*laughing*] You said to listen to my instincts and not mark it!

MARGOT: [*laughing*] Oh, you definitely didn't mark it.

ESTÉE: He thought I was insane.

MARGOT: You hit him really hard.

ESTÉE: It was my first film, and she told me to just go for it.

MARGOT: And then I had to spend the whole night on the phone with his agent.

HUGH: And it never made it into the film?

MARGOT: No, but I have it on a hard drive somewhere.

ESTÉE: You don't?!

MARGOT: I do! I archive all my backup drives, so it'll be somewhere.

Laughter dissipates, the story winds up, they finish their wine.

HUGH: I heard you were doing a play after this. In London?

ESTÉE: [*disinterested*] Yeahhhh, um, I'm gonna do a play called, ah … ? *The Seagull*. With Liam Hemsworth. He's gonna play the writer and I'm gonna play the actress he's so crazy about, it drives him to suicide.

ANNA: Where in London is it playing?

ESTÉE: They told me the name of it … it's one of the big ones …

HUGH: That's so cool.

ANNA: Who's directing?

ESTÉE: Simon.

ANNA: Simon who?

ESTÉE: Ah … I don't know, like … you know, *Simon*? Who … like … does those plays?

HUGH: That is so cool.

ESTÉE: Yeah. I'm excited.

HUGH: Anna, you didn't eat your lasagne?

ANNA: I don't eat meat.

HUGH: You don't eat meat? Well, hand what's left over to this guy.

ESTÉE: So you're vegetarian?

ANNA: Not really.

ESTÉE: Oh, so it's for *health reasons*.

ANNA: For the shoot.

HUGH: I'm the opposite. Like, give me more meat when I'm bulking for a shoot.

ANNA: I would never.

HUGH: Then give me all the meat.

ESTÉE: [*laughing*] Give me all the meat! Ha ha ha! That's so funny!

MARGOT: Look at us all. I knew the three of you would—

She does a hand gesture to imply 'connect'.

HUGH: [*to* ANNA] Well, you're great, you're an icon. [*To* ESTÉE] *But you?* I was intimidated to meet you.

ESTÉE: Me?

HUGH: Yes.

ESTÉE: I'm harmless.

HUGH: I read about your being arrested on set. You assaulted a number of crew members or something? Then the studio cancelled your contract.

ESTÉE: Look … Even if that were true, which I'm not saying it is, it would have cost the studio a small fortune to cancel my contract. And I would have signed a non-disclosure. So who's to say?

HUGH: Right, so *hypothetically* if you assaulted a member of the crew—

ESTÉE: Oh no, that happened. You can find the charges online.

HUGH: So what's hypothetical?

ESTÉE: How much the studio had to pay me to cancel my contract.

MARGOT: You see why I love her?

Beat.

ESTÉE: So Anna, *what happened to you?*

ANNA: What do you mean?

ESTÉE: On {IMDb} it said the last thing you did was *House on the Cul de Sac*. Is that right?

ANNA: Mmmm.

MARGOT: She had a child.

ESTÉE: Oh. How old?

ANNA: Fourteen.

MARGOT: Actually, you look so much like her.

ANNA: Huh?

MARGOT: Your daughter. She looks like Estée, huh? I never noticed before.

ANNA: Now that you mention it …

MARGOT: Her doppelganger, right?

ANNA: Practically the same age and everything. How old are you?

ESTÉE: I'm twenty-four, but I mostly play teenagers. It's really annoying! So you haven't wanted to do any movies or anything that whole time?

ANNA: I've done theatre.

MARGOT: I had to twist her arm to come on board for this. She said no the first four times.

ANNA: It's true.

HUGH: What made you say yes?

ANNA: … I just thought, 'Why not?' It was Margot Visio and I thought, 'Well sure, why not?'

ESTÉE: There are these subreddits that say you're dead.

ANNA: My fans are very creative people.

ESTÉE: Rumour has it the woman in the pap shots is a hired impersonator. They've made all these memes about it. They're really funny, actually. That's how I knew about you for this.

ANNA: Margot said you're a fan?

ESTÉE: She did, did she?

ANNA: That you know my work.

ESTÉE: There's so many *House on the Cul de Sac* remixes on {TikTok}. My remix of your death scene actually got like four million views. I kinda broke the internet.

ANNA *gives* MARGOT *a look.*

HUGH: For me, it's *The Last of the Pretty Ones*. I saw it at the cinema.

MARGOT: One of my favourites. Genre-defining.

ESTÉE: I don't know that one.

ANNA: Well, it's a cult classic.

HUGH: That scene where everyone's gone home after the party. And you're all alone in the house. And you're kinda tipsy. So you go outside for a swim. You strip down to your underwear. And you wade into the water. And all we hear is the sound of the water lapping at the edge of the pool. But then! You hear the stereo switch on inside the house. And it's playing the song we heard earlier. That one that goes—

He sings a bit of it.

MARGOT: No, it's that one that goes—

She sings a bit of it.

HUGH: Oh yeah, yeah you're right!

They both sing a bit of it in unison.

MARGOT: It's like 'their song'.

HUGH: That's right! You and your ex-boyfriend's song. That's how we know there's something weird going on. Because you didn't invite him to the party.

MARGOT: No, he was invited, but he got kicked out because he was acting like a jerk.

HUGH: Anyway you're in the pool, naked—no, wait—in your underwear? And you're pretty sure it's him inside. And you want to go check, but you're also kind of stuck, in case it is him. So you just stay in the pool as still as possible, and hope he doesn't come outside. But then you hear someone open the sliding door. And we're like, 'Oh shit, what's she gonna do?' And you take a deep breath of air and drop down under the surface of the water. And then there is this epic shot from underneath. That's the shot on the main poster right?

ANNA: A variation of, but yeah.

HUGH: It's you underwater with your eyes open. Your hair's floating around you. And you look up to the surface and he's not there, but it's only your point of view. BUT THEN, his head comes into frame!
MARGOT: But he doesn't see her straight away, remember?
HUGH: Yeah yeah yeah! He doesn't see her straight away, so you're holding your breath and holding your breath and then you let this one tiny bubble escape your mouth.
MARGOT: And then she's a goner.
HUGH: Yeah she's a goner from there, because he looks down and you scream, and all these air bubbles fly out of your mouth. So we know for sure you're a goner. And then the drowning scene went on for so long.
ANNA: It was a difficult scene.
MARGOT: One of the best scenes in the film.
HUGH: Horrific to watch, really. You were totally ahead of the genre.
ANNA: I haven't seen it in a long time.
MARGOT: We should watch it.

ANNA *definitely doesn't want to watch it.*

MARGOT *finds her phone and brings up a clip of* ANNA*'s death scene on YouTube. They watch it together as a group.*

ANNA: He was so good. So damn scary.

They watch. We hear ANNA *screaming for her life.*

ESTÉE *stifles a laugh.*

ESTÉE: Sorry. Is it meant to be funny?
MARGOT: Shhhh.
ESTÉE: I mean it's kinda cringe, right?
HUGH: Shhhh.

The clip finishes.

They sit in silence. Then:

HUGH: [*pointing at* ANNA] You know who you remind me of in that?

ANNA *shrugs, 'Who?'*

[*Pointing at* ESTÉE] You!
ANNA: Oh.
ESTÉE: Ha!

HUGH: Not in looks or anything. Just your intensity.
ESTÉE: I get that / a lot.
ANNA: I've never heard that one.
HUGH: You two together are going to be electric.
MARGOT: Anna, we must toast your return to screen.
HUGH: Yes, top me up.
ESTÉE: I'll open another bottle. Anna?
ANNA: No, thank you.
MARGOT: It's good wine. Estée brought it.
ESTÉE: My family owns the vineyard.
ANNA: I'm fine.
MARGOT: Go on. Just a glass with dinner.
ANNA: I'm not drinking.
MARGOT: No, come on now, we must celebrate.
ANNA: I'm good.
MARGOT: Estée, pour her a glass.
HUGH: She said she's not.
MARGOT: One glass won't harm you.
HUGH: Margot?
MARGOT: In fact, I think it might help things.

MARGOT *holds her own glass out for* ANNA *to take.*

HUGH: Margot, don't.
MARGOT: Relax.
HUGH: We are relaxed.

MARGOT *and* ANNA *locked in eye contact.* ANNA *doesn't take the glass.*

MARGOT: That was a test. Excellent work, Anna. [*Putting on a voice*] *You shan't be tempted.*
ESTÉE: So why aren't you drinking? Is it for the shoot too?
ANNA: This industry … I kind of lost grip.
MARGOT: I thought you were so cool back then.
ANNA: I don't see what's so cool about being wasted out of my mind for five years, blowing up every good thing in my life, dropped as soon as I stopped making the studios money, and then stonewalled by all my friends in the business.

Uncomfortable beat.

HUGH: That lasagne was just spectacular.

ESTÉE *spills the wine she's pouring.*

ESTÉE: Oh shit!
ANNA: My script!
ESTÉE: It's not a party until you spill something.
ANNA: All my notes. [*Realising*] My book!

ANNA *holds up her copy of* Frankenstein*, filled diligently with sticky notes and scribbles. The book is soaked with wine.*

ESTÉE: I'm really sorry, Anna.
MARGOT: It's not a problem.
ANNA: Yes, it's a problem; that's all my prep.
ESTÉE: Is there anything I can do?
ANNA: No.

Uncomfortable beat.

Ah, alright. Can I borrow your copy to go over this evening?
ESTÉE: My copy?
ANNA: Of the novel.
ESTÉE: Oh, I don't have a copy.
HUGH: You can take mine.
ANNA: You don't have a copy?
ESTÉE: No.
ANNA: Why not?
ESTÉE: I didn't think I needed one.
HUGH: You can take my copy.
MARGOT: Or mine.
ANNA: You've read it though?
ESTÉE: It's not like an unknown story.
ANNA: But you went back and read it?
ESTÉE: I mean … *I know the gist of it.* Everyone knows the gist, right?
ANNA: You didn't read the source material?

ESTEE *finds this funny.*

ESTÉE: Guilty, Your Honour.
ANNA: You're working with Margot Visio.

MARGOT: Everyone has their process.
ANNA: And Hugh Mirage.
ESTÉE: And they're happy with my work, right?
MARGOT: Of course.
HUGH: Flawless.
ESTÉE: … Great.
ANNA: Seems a little obstinacious.
ESTÉE: Oh, I don't know that word. What does that word mean?
ANNA: Stubborn.
ESTÉE: Oh. Yeah. I am.

Pause.

Any other questions?

Pause.

I'm going for a vape.

ESTÉE *gets up from the table, squeezes past* ANNA.

MARGOT: I'll join you.

ESTÉE *and* MARGOT *leave.* HUGH *and* ANNA *stay at the table.*

HUGH: She's young.
ANNA: *You're young.*
HUGH: I'm a lot older than her.
ANNA: Well, you've trained. And done theatre.
HUGH: Her work's good.
ANNA: A one-trick pony.
HUGH: It's a good trick.
ANNA: I'm not saying she's not a good actor.
HUGH: And strong enough to be around all this bullshit. At her age? And truly not care if people like her.
ANNA: Excuse me for not salivating over an actor still going through puberty.
HUGH: She's not exactly in puberty.
ANNA: Professional puberty, then.

Beat.

Why did you compare her to me?
HUGH: A lot of people compare her to you.

ANNA: Was I that chaotic when I was twenty-four?

HUGH: Well, I didn't know you at twenty-four, but I'm almost certain she's worse.

ANNA: What makes you say that?

HUGH: Have you googled her? The digital trail is … vivid. It won't take you long to find the problematic rants and OnlyFans videos.

ANNA: Sounds like you've googled her.

HUGH: I google everyone.

ANNA: You google yourself?

HUGH: Obviously.

ANNA: You google me?

HUGH: Of course.

ANNA: What did you find?

HUGH: Some subreddits about you being dead.

ANNA: Screw you.

Beat.

She called my work cringe.

HUGH: Fuck her. What would she know? Plus, horror these days has gone way too highbrow.

ANNA: Right? Thank you.

HUGH: Gimme the C-list actors, the cringe dialogue, the predictable plot points and just scare the shit outta me. You know? It shouldn't be that hard.

ANNA: Yes. *Thank you.*

HUGH: People don't want elevated, prestige cinema, or clever takes on hot-button topics.

ANNA: I'm sorry, but do we only make scary movies for smart people now?

HUGH: Well, we're not doing scary, remember? We're doing 'gothic'.

ANNA: No, no, no, we're doing 'European'.

HUGH: How could I forget.

Beat.

ANNA: You like the script?

HUGH: It's okay.

ANNA: Just okay?

HUGH: It's like, there's so much in the book. Why would you choose the baby parallel, you know? There's just something about it I don't like …

ANNA: Because it's about women.

HUGH: No, it's not that. Like, what's so original about the novel is she invented a whole literary genre. She's literally the creator of science fiction. But focusing on the mother-daughter thing? It reduces it for me.

ANNA: Because it's about women.

HUGH: No, that's not it. It's something, but that's not it.

ANNA: Well, it's only a mother-daughter thing if you believe she's the daughter.

HUGH: She's obviously the daughter.

ANNA: … Sure.

HUGH: You don't think she's her daughter?

ANNA: I think if we believe Angelica, and Elsa's making it all up, then it's not a motherhood parallel at all. It's about how we pathologise and project onto female artists.

Beat.

I will need to borrow your copy of the novel this evening, if that's okay?

HUGH: It's in my room.

Slow beat. Is this an invitation?

ANNA: … So go get it.

HUGH: Right now?

ANNA: Go on.

HUGH: …

ANNA: You know where your room is?

HUGH: I know where your room is.

ANNA: Get outta here.

HUGH *goes to leave.*

HUGH: Estée's rough around the edges. But the two of you together? That could really be something. Let her in a little.

ANNA *sits alone. She studies the sides, annoyed they're now soaked with wine.*

ESTÉE *returns to get the bottle of wine. She leans over* ANNA *to grab it.*

ESTÉE: [*in a faux-French accent*] Pardonne-moi, en passant. (Excuse me, coming through.)

ANNA: Estée?

ESTÉE: Oui oui? (Yes?)

ANNA: I wanted to ask you: here, in this scene where I get on my knees and beg you not to kill him?

ESTÉE: Yeah.

ANNA: You sort of rush through it without even looking at me. If you could pause for a second, and make eye contact with me first, my distress would last longer. The way you're playing it, Angelica is sort of powerless.

ESTÉE: … Uh-huh.

ANNA: I think holding it longer, and looking at me, before you make a decision, would really play well.

ESTÉE: … Yeah. Sure.

ANNA: If you just caught my eyes for a second.

ESTÉE: I can do that.

ANNA: We want this to be 'wow', you know?

ESTÉE: That's what I want.

ANNA: Me too.

ESTÉE: I'm having some difficulty. Are you feeling it too?

ANNA: Well, you're a little green, but you did that hard scene this morning and you were really good.

ESTÉE: I guess I'm nervous.

ANNA: Of what?

ESTÉE: The disconnect.

ANNA: In terms of the character?

ESTÉE: No, in terms of you.

ANNA: Me?

ESTÉE: Your reaction just now, when I hadn't read the book?

ANNA: Oh, that?

ESTÉE: You got upset and I could feel this wall go up. I can still feel it. When, right now, we needed to be—

She does the same hand gesture as MARGOT *to imply 'connecting'.*

ANNA: I was judgey. I can be like that.

ESTÉE: I want to give you the best performance I can. No holding back.

ANNA: That's what I want.

ESTÉE: Great.

ANNA: Go all the way.

ESTÉE: Like you in that drowning scene. That was like, 'wow'. How'd you tap into that?

ANNA: … I dunno. Just like, off my face probably. I was pretty fucked up.

ESTÉE: You're an amazing actor when you're fucked up.

ANNA: (WTF … ?)

ESTÉE: Just saying.

ANNA: You know I used to be the front-page tabloid party girl everyone was scared of.

ESTÉE: You're scared of me?

ANNA: Not me, no. But I can sense the others are a little.

ESTÉE: Compliment accepted.

ANNA: Hey, fun secret about that film. Me and one of the camera men were hooking up the entire shoot.

ESTÉE: You're as bad as me.

ANNA: I'm sure I was worse.

ESTÉE: *I dunno.*

ANNA: Things were pretty crazy back then.

ESTÉE: *I dunno.* I could tell you some stories.

ANNA: Oh, get this, so, during the shoot, me and the camera guy were … like I said. And I missed a period. I thought it was me, you know? The pills, and the drinking, and the skipping meals. Sometimes that can mess with, you know, your stuff. But no. I was pregnant. Then … I don't know if the stress was—I mean, *I blame the stress*. And the conditions of the set. And what the director put us through. Anyway, I was pregnant. And then one morning, the morning we were filming the drowning scene, I wasn't anymore. And I just went, like, full monster on set.

ESTÉE: [*gentle*] Oh my God, Anna. Did you tell anyone?

ANNA: My performance was the most important thing, *and the distress was working,* so I didn't really think about it much at the time.

ESTÉE: That's really triggering.

ANNA: Sorry, that got a little—

ESTÉE: No. I mean, yes. It's dark. But it's good.

ANNA: Yeah?

ESTÉE: Yeah. That's actual trauma.

ANNA: Oh. No. Things were different then.

ESTÉE: You have really leaky boundaries.
ANNA: Ha! *That's what my daughter keeps telling me.*
ESTÉE: Have you ever talked to a professional?
ANNA: I didn't need to.
ESTÉE: That's your protective mechanisms talking.
ANNA: I don't think so.
ESTÉE: Trust me. I've done the work.
ANNA: … Well, thanks for listening.
ESTÉE: Of course. *I'm an empath.*

Beat.

ANNA: Don't repeat that to anyone. I don't even know why I—
ESTÉE: You have a beautiful girl now, right?
ANNA: Yes. Well, she's not a girl. Fourteen. She's almost an adult.
ESTÉE: What's her name?
ANNA: Tessa.
ESTÉE: *Tessa.* So pretty.
ANNA: She follows you online. She wants to be an actor.
ESTÉE: *Bless.*
ANNA: She showed me your TikToks. She really wanted me to do this with you. So I did.
ESTÉE: What's her handle?
ANNA: I don't know.
ESTÉE: She have your last name?
ANNA: Yeah.
ESTÉE: Found her. She's cute. I'll have to follow her back.
ANNA: That's okay, you don't have to—
ESTÉE: Followed.

Beat.

Night, Anna.

ESTÉE *goes to leave,* ANNA *calls her back.*

ANNA: So what's your thing?
ESTÉE: What's my thing?
ANNA: You said you're even worse than me. You could 'tell me some stories'.
ESTÉE: *Oh …* Yeah, no, I don't think I have anything like that.

ANNA: Come on.

ESTÉE: Really.

ANNA: There's no way you don't have a story.

ESTÉE: What do you mean?

ANNA: I mean, look at you.

ESTÉE: Look at me?

ANNA: You're interesting. You must have an interesting story.

ESTÉE: Why would I have an interesting story?

ANNA: Because looking at you, you're clearly, you know, not the usual choice.

ESTÉE: … Why would you say that?

ANNA: *Well, you know how it is these days.*

ESTÉE: No, how is it these days?

ANNA: It doesn't matter how good of an actor you are. You need to bring something else to the table.

ESTÉE: … Uh-huh.

ANNA: That goes for everyone, I mean. Like, I bring, um, what do I bring?

ESTÉE: I honestly don't know.

ANNA: Well, I bring … continuity! It's comforting for people.

ESTÉE: And I'm *not* comforting, for people?

ANNA: Not at all. You're a disruption.

ESTÉE: *Wow.*

ANNA: It's a good thing. It's a far more interesting choice.

ESTÉE: …

ANNA: *I'm saying it's a good thing.* It's about time things changed.

ESTÉE: I agree.

ANNA: …

ESTÉE: It's not all about you anymore, huh?

ANNA: No. *No way.* I don't need all the attention, that's what I'm saying.

ESTÉE: …

ANNA: You know what I'm saying, right?

ESTÉE: Sure. I'll tell you all the boxes I tick and you'll decide if I deserve to be here.

ANNA: No, sorry, you've completely misunderstood me.

ESTÉE: Have I?

ANNA: That's pretty much the opposite of what I'm saying.

ESTÉE: Oh. So you weren't suggesting I have some sort of interesting story about the barriers I've overcome that make me an 'edgy choice' for this film.

ANNA: … No.

ESTÉE: Well, that's a relief. Otherwise you would have really put your foot in it.

Uncomfortable beat.

ANNA: To be clear, I think you're great.

ANNA*'s phone rings; it's Tessa.* ESTÉE *catches the start of the call.*

[*Taking the call*] Hi darling. Wow, she did huh? … No I didn't ask her to … Well, your mom still has some social credit … Oh? Ah, no I don't think she can—

ESTÉE: Want me to say hi?

ANNA: [*to* ESTÉE, *whispering*] You don't have to.

ESTÉE: It's fine.

ANNA: [*on the phone*] We were actually just having dinner together. Should I put her on?

ANNA *passes* ESTÉE *the phone.*

ESTÉE: [*on the phone*] Is that Tessa? … Hiiiiiiii … Your mom is so OTT … I'm lowkey learning so much just watching her.

ESTÉE *finds a corner and continues talking to Tessa.* ANNA *watches on.*

HUGH *returns from his room with the book.*

[*On the phone*] Hey, maybe you could help me with my character, huh? Whaddaya say?

HUGH: Got the book. If you could just leave the sticky notes where they are.

ESTÉE: [*on the phone*] So I'm playing your mom's biggest stan, and I want you to tell me literally everything about her as a mother.

ANNA *watches* ESTÉE. *She feels uneasy.*

HUGH: *Anna?*

ANNA: Huh?

HUGH: The novel?

ANNA: Oh, yeah.

Pause.

No, I'm good.

SCENE FOUR

On set again to reshoot the confrontation between ANGELICA *and* ANNA.

What was an early morning call has now pushed way out as ANNA *has been a no-show. The team is running behind. Everyone is frustrated.*

ANNA *arrives.*

ESTÉE: [*fake-polite*] Morning, Anna.
HUGH: Look who finally showed.
ANNA: I've been in wardrobe.
HUGH: Margot's looking for you.
ANNA: That make-up girl is a nightmare.
ESTÉE: Jenny.
ANNA: I looked completely washed-out.
HUGH: Your call time was two hours ago.
ANNA: Hey, be honest, does Estée always look better than us?
HUGH: Margot's furious.
ANNA: No, I looked *completely* washed-out. Trust me. It was worth the wait.

MARGOT *enters.*

MARGOT: We've been standing around waiting.
ANNA: Margot, thank goodness. I can't work with that make-up girl. I had to make her do the entire look again.
MARGOT: We're behind schedule.
ANNA: Pffff, ten minutes or so.
MARGOT: It said six on the callsheet.
ANNA: My call time was eight.
MARGOT: It was eight on the old callsheet. The new time was six.
ANNA: I didn't get a new callsheet.
MARGOT: You would have been given it.
ANNA: I don't know what to tell you. I didn't get a callsheet.

MARGOT: You've wasted hours of our time. If you could please apologise to the crew, we can get going.

ANNA: *I've been stuck in wardrobe.* If you'd seen it, trust me, you would have sent me straight back.

MARGOT: We radioed wardrobe; they said you weren't there.

ANNA: Then they lied because that's where I've been for hours.

MARGOT: [*calling out to the group*] Okay, crew! So sorry for the delay. Actors are good to go now. Going back to yesterday's scene—Scene Twenty-Three-A—for Anna's coverage.

ANNA: [*interrupting*] I can't work with that make-up girl anymore. I want who's doing Estée.

MARGOT: What?

ANNA: Estée's make-up artist. I need them doing me.

MARGOT: Estée's person is doing Estée.

ANNA: Why don't I get my own person?

MARGOT: You have Jenny.

ANNA: Well, she's shit!

MARGOT: Anna, you're giving me a headache.

ANNA: Honestly. She's terrible. I'm sorry, but it's true.

MARGOT: [*calling out*] Twenty-Three-A last looks.

ANNA: Twenty-Three-A? Aren't we doing the new sides?

MARGOT: They've been scrapped.

ANNA: I stayed up memorising them.

MARGOT: You'd know they'd been scrapped if you read the new callsheet. [*Calling out*] Positions for Twenty-Three-A. Going in five!

ANNA: I haven't prepped Twenty-Three-A.

MARGOT: [*to the actors*] Okay team, we've done this already, you know the blocking, I know it's going to be excellent.

ESTÉE: You want anything different from yesterday?

MARGOT: No. Exactly the same.

ANNA: Exactly the same?

MARGOT: It's your close-up, Anna. So now's your chance to go for it if you feel a different impulse.

ANNA: So what do you want me to do?

MARGOT: Do whatever your character would do. React, respond. [*Gesturing to* ESTÉE] It's all in her, yeah? Find whatever it is *you do, in her.*

MARGOT *exits the frame. The actors prepare themselves.*

ESTÉE: Happy to keep things the same?

ANNA: Thanks for talking to my daughter, that was so nice of you.

ESTÉE: Oh, it's no problem.

ANNA: It meant a lot to her.

Beat.

You look so pretty by the way. Your skin.

ESTÉE: Hydrate hydrate hydrate.

ANNA: Hey, do I look washed-out under these lights?

ESTÉE: So, happy to keep things as is?

ANNA: Totally. So far, your work has been flawless. I was surprised you hadn't done any prep.

ESTÉE: Oh, I prepared.

ANNA: I mean research.

ESTÉE: I've done my research.

ANNA: You didn't read the novel.

ESTÉE: [*sweetly*] No, Anna. I researched you.

ANNA: My movies, you mean?

ESTÉE: Elsa's obsessed with Angelica, right? So you're my source material. I know everything about you.

FIRST AD: Quiet on set! Let's turnover.

ESTÉE *finds her mark.* ANNA *follows.*

Roll sound.

SOUND: Sound speed.

FIRST AD: Roll camera.

DP: Rolling.

FIRST AD: Mark it.

FIRST AD, SOUND, DP, CLAPPER *and* 2ND AC *can be seen or unseen.*

CLAPPER: Scene Twenty-Three-A, take six.

Sound of a clapper board.

FIRST AD: Set?

DP: Yes, set.

MARGOT: Action!

The actors speak once again in their Act One accents.

ANGELICA: Who are you? Why are you in my home?

ELSA: Come on. You know who I am, Angelica.

ANGELICA: No, I don't.

ELSA: If you had to guess.

ANGELICA: I have no idea.

ELSA: You're being coy now?

ANGELICA: [*stumbling on her line*] You need to—to tell me who you are, or I'll call the police.

ELSA: It should be obvious.

Uncomfortable pause.

ANGELICA/ANNA: Sorry, LINE?

FIRST AD: 'Fine. The police can tell me who you are.'

MARGOT: Keep rolling!

ANGELICA: Fine. The police can tell me who you are.

ELSA: It's me. It's Clara.

Uncomfortable pause.

ANGELICA/ANNA: Sorry, LINE?

MARGOT: CUT!

MARGOT *enters the frame.*

ANNA: Sorry! Sorry, that was me.

MARGOT: What happened?

ANNA: Can I see the script again?

Someone begrudgingly hands her a folder she could probably reach herself.

MARGOT: Let's go again.

ANNA: [*reading out loud*] 'You need to tell me who you are, or I'll call the police.' 'It should be obvious.' 'Fine, the police can tell me who you are.' 'It's me. It's Clara.' 'Did somebody put you up to this?' Yep yep yep. Got it.

MARGOT: [*calling out*] Going again!

MARGOT *exits the frame.* ESTÉE *and* ANNA *find their mark and prepare themselves.*

FIRST AD: Quiet on set! Turning over. Roll sound.

SOUND: Sound speed.

FIRST AD: Roll camera.

DP: Rolling.

FIRST AD: Mark it.

CLAPPER: Scene Twenty-Three-A, take seven.

Sound of a clapper board.

FIRST AD: Set?

DP: Set.

MARGOT: Action!

ANGELICA: Who are you? Why are you in my home?

ELSA: Come on. You know who I am, Angelica.

ANGELICA: No, I don't.

ELSA: If you had to guess.

ANNA, *as* ANGELICA, *feels the moment. She goes to speak then stops herself, she thinks again.*

FIRST AD: 'I have no idea.'

ANNA: No. I know my line! I was— Screw it. I need to cut.

MARGOT: No, keep going.

ANNA: I need to cut!

MARGOT: Keep rolling.

ANGELICA: I have no idea.

ELSA: You're being coy now?

ANGELICA: You need to tell me who you are, or I'll call the police.

ELSA: [*off-script*] You can't even say it.

ANGELICA/ANNA: [*off-script*] Say what?

ELSA: [*off-script*] My name!

ANGELICA: Fine. The police can tell me who you are.

ELSA: [*off-script*] It's me. It's Tessa.

ANGELICA: Did somebody put you up to this?

ELSA: You didn't answer my letters.

ANGELICA: Listen, Elsa.

ELSA: [*off-script*] Tessa.

ANGELICA: Elsa, I've had your type before.

ELSA: [*off-script*] I look so much like you.

ANGELICA: That's not? No—

ELSA: [*off-script*] I want to be an actor.

ANGELICA/ANNA: Sorry, LINE?

MARGOT: CUT!

MARGOT *enters the playing space.*

What? What happened?

ANNA: Those weren't the lines.

MARGOT: Just run with it.

ANNA: I thought we were doing it exactly the same.

ESTÉE: I could feel I wasn't affecting you, so I wanted to 'RAHHH!' at you, you know?

ANNA: It's just that 'Tessa' is my actual daughter's name.

ESTÉE: That's why I said it.

ANNA: That's a bit of a boundary for me.

MARGOT: We don't have to use that line in the final edit. We're just filming your reactions.

ANNA: Right. *Right, of course.* [*To* ESTÉE] Let's mark what you want to change.

MARGOT: No. Don't mark it. The creature is free. Above everything: she's unpredictable. Let's go again.

Beat.

[*Calling out*] Going again!

MARGOT *exits the frame.* ANNA *and* ESTÉE *find their mark.*

FIRST AD: Quiet on Set! Turning over. Roll sound.

SOUND: Sound speed.

FIRST AD: Roll camera.

DP: Rolling.

FIRST AD: Mark it.

CLAPPER: Scene Twenty-Three-A, take eight.

Sound of clapper board.

FIRST AD: Set?

DP: Set.

MARGOT: Action!

ANGELICA: Who are you? Why are you in my home?

ELSA: Come on. You know who I am, Angelica.

ANGELICA: No, I don't.

ELSA: If you had to guess.

ANGELICA: I have no idea.

ELSA: You're being coy now?

ANGELICA: You need to tell me who you are, or I'll call the police.

ELSA: [*off-script*] You can't even say it.

ANGELICA/ANNA: [*off-script*] Say what?

ELSA: [*off-script*] My name!

ANGELICA: Fine. The police can tell me who you are.

ELSA: [*off-script*] It's me. It's Tessa.

ANGELICA: Did somebody put you up to this?

ELSA: You didn't answer my letters.

ANGELICA: Listen, Elsa.

ELSA: [*off-script*] Tessa.

ANGELICA: Elsa, I've had your type before.

ELSA: [*off-script*] I look so much like you.

ANGELICA: You're not the first journalist to make up stories like this.

ELSA: [*off-script*] I'll tell everyone what you did.

ANGELICA: I'll call you a taxi.

ELSA: [*off-script*] That you chose a film over a child.

ANGELICA: [*off-script*] Get back!

ELSA: [*off-script, off blocking*] All that sacrifice and now your movies aren't even relevant.

ANGELICA: [*off-script*] No, I—

ELSA: [*off-script, off blocking*] I'm embarrassed to call you my mother.

ANGELICA/ANNA: … So, so, do I move over here now?

MARGOT: CUT!

MARGOT *enters the frame.*

MARGOT: What's going on!?

ESTÉE: That one felt good.

MARGOT: Why is this scene so polite all of a sudden?

ESTÉE: I can go harder.

MARGOT: [*to* ANNA] You need a hot cocoa? Blanket around your shoulders?

ANNA: No?

MARGOT: Then trust the process!

Uncomfortable pause which no-one wants to fill.

ANNA: It's hard to trust the process when things keep changing.

ESTÉE: I thought that one was good.

ANNA: So what do you want me to do?

MARGOT: I need to see you go there.

ANNA: Uh-huh. Do you know specifically where you want to see me go?

MARGOT: To wherever it is in your psyche that scares the shit out of you.

ANNA: Okay.

MARGOT: What haunts you, Anna?

ANNA: … I don't think I have anything.

MARGOT: I've seen it in your work. Your early movies. You were in so much pain.

ANNA: I wasn't in pain, I was out of my fucking mind.

MARGOT: Then let's get you to that place again. What were the steps?

ANNA: I mean I was pretty much always completely out of it … And they'd put the camera on me … And I'd, like, humiliate myself … And that was kinda perfect.

MARGOT: *Uh-huh.*

ANNA: (WTF … ?)

MARGOT: You wanna try accessing that trauma.

ANNA: I wasn't accessing trauma.

MARGOT: You created trauma in your performance though.

ANNA: I mean, it might have read as trauma.

MARGOT: And thinking about it now: that's awful. Don't you feel angry? Taken advantage of?

ANNA: No.

MARGOT: But you were.

ANNA: No, I don't feel that way.

Beat.

MARGOT: [*suddenly angry*] I'm sorry, are you even willing to be directed?

ANNA: Yes?

MARGOT: Then stop standing there like a fucking void.

Tense pause.

You think I care if that sounds mean? Good. Use it.

Tense pause.

ESTÉE: I have an / idea.

ANNA: What if I / tried—

ESTÉE: Oh, sorry.

ANNA: No, you go first.

ESTÉE*'s cautious but proceeds.*

ESTÉE: We can do more to make it real. Between you and me, Anna, I mean. So it's less performancey.

MARGOT: Good.

ESTÉE: Use what you hate about me and let it fester and bubble up.

ANNA: I don't hate you.

ESTÉE: You can say it. I don't care.

ANNA: I don't.

ESTÉE: That's what I'm doing with you.

ANNA: *Okay.*

MARGOT: Of course there are things to hate about Estée. Look at her. She's talented, she's young, she's in demand. She's rich now, very rich, and powerful. Her performance is completely free. And, well, she's you. She's the exact girl you used to be.

ESTÉE: The critics'll weigh in. They'll compare us. And not just what you do in this movie. But your acting back then too. I'm coming for your crown.

ANNA: [*eye-rolling*] Oh my God.

MARGOT: She's giving you gold. React. Respond!

ANNA: I am responding. I feel like, to me, who Angelica is, is, held. She's got self respect. She isn't going to give Elsa what she wants because that's admitting—emotionally at least—that she's getting to her. And I think she's smarter than that. That's my character.

MARGOT: [*considering, slowly, working through it*] Mmmm. Okay, okay. So you don't want to react, because you don't want to show her that she's getting to you? But the thing is: she is getting to you. The thought of the Creature, out there, psychologically torments Victor.

ANNA: Right.

MARGOT: So we need to see you unravel.

ANNA: Angelica needs to unravel.

MARGOT: You need to unravel.

ANNA: As my character.

MARGOT: I don't see a separation. I want this, this *charge*. This terrifying electricity between you two. [*To* ESTÉE] You want a confession from her? Get a confession! You want to get in her face?

She gets close to ESTÉE*'s face.*

Get up in her face. [*To* ANNA] And you, this girl's sent letters, she's found your address. She's tracked you down. She's broken into your home. She's dangerous. You want her gone? Get her out!

ANNA: Get her out.

MARGOT: Let's go again. Yes?

They both nod.

[*Calling out*] Going again!

They reset.

FIRST AD: Quiet on Set! Turning over. Roll sound.

SOUND: Sound speed.

FIRST AD: Roll camera.

DP: Rolling.

FIRST AD: Mark it.

CLAPPER: Scene Twenty-Three-A, take nine.

Sound of clapper board.

FIRST AD: Set?

DP: Set.

MARGOT: Action!

Lightning.

The world distorts.

CLAPPER: Scene Twenty-Three-A, take ten.
Take sixteen.
Take twenty-eight.
Take forty-one.
Take fifty-four.
Take sixty-seven.
Take eighty.
Take ninety-two.

Take one hundred and four.

The loud ring of a sound stage bell.

Heightened, this scene swirls straight into:

SCENE FIVE

ANNA: [*on the phone to her agent*] I thought it over and I can't! … Replace me! … So I'm a hostage? … Figure something out.

MARGOT *appears.* ANNA *hangs up.*

Margot.

MARGOT: Everything okay?

ANNA: I want out.

MARGOT: In the middle of production?

ANNA: This is humiliating.

MARGOT: That means we're getting somewhere.

ANNA: I'm not doing that scene again!

MARGOT: Well, that's not your call to make.

ANNA: I've run it a hundred times.

MARGOT: And it's not working.

ANNA: *I'm* not working.

MARGOT: There are a number of things that aren't working—

ANNA: What else is it then? What what / what?

MARGOT: You're not committed. In a film like this, you can't fake it.

ANNA: I've worked with a million more experienced directors, on much *much* bigger sets than this, and no-one has ever had the disrespect to tell me I'm not committed.

MARGOT: So commit! Huh? What's the problem?

ANNA: It's Estée. She's …

MARGOT: Estée's what?

ANNA: I don't think it's good for us to work together.

MARGOT: Estée's the real deal. She's a serious actor.

ANNA: I'm a serious actor.

MARGOT *scoffs.*

Why is that funny?

MARGOT: …

ANNA: I've won awards.

MARGOT: MTV Awards.

ANNA: Sorry, as opposed to … ?

MARGOT: *I don't need to win awards to prove—*

ANNA: Ohhh, your European festival circuits. *Right.* Much cooler and much more serious.

MARGOT: Your films had sequels.

ANNA: People love sequels.

MARGOT: Sequels aren't serious though.

ANNA: You don't take me seriously?

MARGOT: Honestly, it's the genre that's thwarting you. Your performance hasn't modernised with it.

ANNA: Then why'd you cast me?

MARGOT: Because I believe I can pull a serious performance out of you.

ANNA: Oh, that's so kind of you. No, thank you for that.

MARGOT: And you across from Estée says something bigger than your performance.

ANNA: Wow, no, that's so clever of you.

MARGOT: Because the monster isn't a hideous monster. The monster is something made in your image that starts surpassing you.

ANNA: And by 'monster', you mean?

MARGOT: Estée, obviously.

ANNA: Obviously.

MARGOT: Maybe what my script needs from you is beyond what you're capable of.

ANNA: Maybe I'm used to working with a different calibre of director.

MARGOT: … Uh-huh.

ANNA: Maybe you're the one out of your depth. Because everyone agrees I'm a great actor.

MARGOT: Alright. Should we be real with each other for a second?

ANNA: Please.

MARGOT: *The Last of the Pretty Ones* wasn't very good. You were iconic. And I'm a fan of your work. But you weren't 'good' in it.

ANNA: It's a cult classic.

MARGOT: It's *become* a cult classic, yes. And you're an icon. But was it actually good? No, not really. So if me being out of my depth is trying to resurrect the career of someone who was never very good in the first place, then sure, maybe that's a part of what's going on here.

Tense pause.

ANNA: I'm out. I'm backing out. I'll pay whatever studio fine they send me. I don't care.

MARGOT: Anna, stop. You walk away from this and you're done. No-one will touch you.

ANNA: What's new?

MARGOT: You leave, you're over. You're dead.

ANNA: I've been dead a long time.

MARGOT: I mean it. I had to beg the studio to bring you on board. Prove to them you're a serious actor. Prove it to everyone. The fans. The sceptics. To me. Prove it to your daughter.

ANNA: Margot, I can't give you what you want. I thought I could, but I can't.

Frustrated, MARGOT *takes a seat.*

MARGOT *knows* ANNA*'s right. It's not working.*

Silence. MARGOT *gives it one last shot.*

MARGOT: For what it's worth, I could, you know, arrange help for you, after this is all done.

ANNA: What do you mean?

MARGOT: I mean if you need to find a way to decompress. So you can access what you need to access. No-one here will talk. We'll pay for whatever help you need to get back to earth, safely, in time for the red carpet.

ANNA: My characters don't wash away afterwards. I don't feel safe for months.

MARGOT: Fuck safety. You want to make safe art?

Pause. ANNA *considers.*

ANNA: I should have taken that reality show they offered me.

MARGOT: Maybe.

ANNA: It was on an island.

Pause.

MARGOT: Whatever it takes, you know? The art has to come first.

ANNA *accepts.* MARGOT *leaves for the night, but turns back to* ANNA *just before she departs.*

You know this is all on your terms, right?

ANNA *nods.*

ANNA *finds her script and* Frankenstein *novel and sets up at the table. She opens it to the section she's working on. She says a few of* ESTÉE*'s lines.*

ANNA: [*as* ESTÉE] 'I'm curious to know: are those scenes from your early films real? Did you do all those things?' Yeah, bitch. 'I don't know how you'd come up with that stuff if it hadn't happened to you.'

Frustrated, ANNA *gets up to grab a bottle of wine and a wine glass.*

She pours herself a drink. Drinks it in one go. Then pours another, way beyond a standard pour.

She closes her eyes and says the dialogue to herself. It's gentle and heartfelt.

[*As* ESTÉE] 'I don't know how you'd come up with that stuff if it hadn't happened to you.'

In some way, the space shifts to a more heightened, theatrical realm.

After a minute she goes to the gun safe. She takes out the pistol. She examines it.

She raises it to mock firing it.

[*Whispering, pretending to shoot*] Pchhhhhh.

ESTÉE *enters.*

ANNA *hides the gun and busies herself in the novel.*

ESTÉE: You need to run lines or something?

ANNA: Are you fucking with me right now?

ESTÉE: No.

ANNA: You're very hard to read, you know that?

ESTÉE: I get that all the time. But I don't think that's true. I actually think I'm so easy to read that people overthink me.

Pause.

You know there's something I've really been wanting to ask you.

ANNA: …

ESTÉE: Is it amazing being as famous as you are?

ANNA: No. I actually find it kind of horrific to try and be that person again.

ESTÉE *smiles at her.*

ESTÉE: All this energy to find her. Resurrect her. When really I think you want that version of you dead. Fuck that version. Kill her. Do better. But for real this time.

ANNA: Kill her for real.

ESTÉE: That's just my opinion.

ESTÉE *leaves.*

ANNA *feels the weight of the gun in her hands.*

SCENE SIX

On set. Reshooting ELSA*'s discovery of* ANGELICA *and* HENRICK *mid-roleplay.*

ANNA, ESTÉE *and* HUGH *wait on set for* MARGOT *who is taking a phone call.*

ANNA*'s wasted. She eats leftover lasagne out of a container.* ANNA *is 'in accent' the entire scene.*

MARGOT *finishes her phone call and joins the group.*

MARGOT: So … I know we've spent the morning setting up for Scene Twenty-Six-B … But I just got off the phone with our producer. The studio's reviewed the footage, and what we have is good enough. Which means we're moving forward. That's a wrap on Scene Twenty-Six-B. [*Calling out*] Crew, let's get externals while we have everyone.

ANNA: [*in accent as* ANGELICA] Is this some funny joke?

ESTÉE *and* HUGH *go find jackets.* ANNA *doesn't move.*

MARGOT: [*calling out*] So for the externals, I want to make sure we get the facade of the house at sundown—

ANNA: Margot Margot Margot listennnnnnnn. *I'm ready to go.* You know?

MARGOT: You can drop the accent, Anna. [*Calling out*] Can I get scaffolding in?

ANNA: Stop! Everyone stop! She's just messing with me! Trying to get me off guard and out of nowhere she'll be like, 'ACTION!'

MARGOT: [*calling out*] And can we get Anna some coffee, please?

ANNA: Margot, please? It's my big scene. It's my moment. Just give me one take.

MARGOT: The studio's called it. It's out of my hands.

ANNA: *That's bullshit!*

MARGOT: [*calling out*] Where's that coffee for Anna?

ESTÉE: Anna, I'll get you some black coffee, babe. Yeah?

ANNA: [*to* MARGOT] Listen listen listen. I'm good for the scene. Okay? *You understand what I'm saying?* I'm good for it.

HUGH: We can do one take, right? We're good for it. Estée?

ESTÉE: Whatever.

MARGOT: *One take?*

ANNA: That's all I need.

Pause.

MARGOT: [*calling out*] Okay, everyone! Pause there. We're doing *one final take only* of Scene Twenty-Six-B before externals.

FIRST AD: Alright everyone, last look, then reset to first position.

MARGOT: [*calling out*] No stopping. Keep it moving, keep it fluid, see what happens.

ESTÉE: [*handing* ANNA *coffee*] Here you go, hun.

ANNA: Your TikTok impression of me was shit.

MARGOT *gets the pistol out of the prop box for* ESTÉE.

MARGOT: [*to* ESTÉE] We don't have ballistics, so no firing the gun.

ESTÉE: No worries. So it's not loaded?

MARGOT: It's not loaded, but insurance-wise, you can't fire the gun on set without ballistics here.

ESTÉE: Got it.

MARGOT: Just mark it without firing, you know, hold it up, they fall over, so we can cut between takes if we need to.

ESTÉE *sets the pistol.*

And you know what? This is our last chance to play around—so let's throw everything up in the air and see where it lands.

ESTÉE: Yeah, that's cool.

MARGOT: See where you can take it.

ANNA, ESTÉE *and* HUGH *find their mark and prepare themselves.*

MARGOT: So, actors, we're gonna take it from, 'Tell me you're a monster.'

ANNA *is on her mark, fully focused and ready to go, but still holding the container of lasagne.*

Anna?

ANNA: …

MARGOT: Anna?

ANNA: I heard you!

MARGOT: Great.

MARGOT *takes the food off* ANNA *on her way out of frame.*

FIRST AD: Quiet on Set! Let's turn over! Roll sound.

SOUND: Sound speed.

FIRST AD: Roll camera.

DP: Rolling.

ANNA: Wait! Whose coverage is this?

MARGOT: It's roaming.

FIRST AD: Mark it.

CLAPPER: Scene Twenty-Six-B, take thirteen.

Sound of clapper board.

FIRST AD: Set?

DP: Yes, set.

FIRST AD: And …

MARGOT: Whenever you're ready!

A long pause. All eyes are on ANNA *who takes an uncomfortably long amount of time to say her first line. She realises the others are waiting for her.*

ANNA: What? Did you say 'Action'?

MARGOT: Oh my God! Yes! Action!

ANNA: Is it me? Sorry! Line?

FIRST AD: 'Tell me you're a monster.'

ANNA: That's my line?

MARGOT: Yes.

ANNA: No wonder I didn't remember it.

FIRST AD: Take thirteen. Still rolling!

They all speak once again in their Part One accents.

ANGELICA: 'Tell me you're a monster.'
HENRICK: 'I'm a monster'
ANGELICA: 'Will you harm me?'
HENRICK: 'If that's your desire.'
ANGELICA: 'I desire your darkness. Unleash it upon me!'
HENRICK: 'As you wish.'
ANGELICA: 'I won't submit easily.'
HENRICK: He's excited now.
ANGELICA: 'Chase me then, you monster.'
HENRICK: 'You want a monster? I'll show you a monster.'

A shadow in the doorway, and ELSA *appears, unnoticed by* ANGELICA *and* HENRICK.

'Get back here.'
ANGELICA: 'Stay away!'
HENRICK: 'You can't run from me, Angelica.'
ANGELICA: She reaches the front door. [*Trying the handle*] But it's locked!
HENRICK: He closes in.
ANGELICA: She's out of breath.
HENRICK: 'I have you cornered now.'
ANGELICA: 'What are you going to do to me?'
HENRICK: 'What I've been longing for.'
ANGELICA: 'Are you going to *kill me*?'
HENRICK: 'Yes. I'm going to kill you.'

ELSA *picks up the pistol. She raises it to shoot* HENRICK.

ELSA: STOP!
ANGELICA: Clara?!
ELSA: [*aiming it at* HENRICK] Get away from her!
HENRICK: Whoa whoa whoa, it's just a game.
ELSA: Let her go.
HENRICK: Just a silly 'monster in the house' game we like to play.
ANGELICA: Clara, what are you—?
ELSA: [*to* HENRICK] You! Get over there.
ANGELICA: Clara, it's alright.
HENRICK: It's all just pretending.
ELSA: Get away from her or I shoot.

HENRICK *releases* ANGELICA.

ANGELICA: It's not real. He wasn't actually trying to kill me.

ELSA *aims the pistol at* HENRICK*'s head.*

HENRICK: Whoa! Careful where you point that thing, huh. Okay. Um, can I ask you a question?

ELSA: Fire away.

HENRICK: Ah, how'd you get in here?

ELSA: The key was in the electrical box with your bike lock.

HENRICK: Right. I didn't think of that.

ANGELICA: Shall we have a drink?

Totally off-script at this point, ANNA, *as* ANGELICA, *moves to make a drink.*

You want a drink Clara? The good stuff. Screw it. Why not? Ice?

ELSA: [*still gripping the gun*] No thanks.

ANGELICA: Henrick? You want a drink?

HENRICK: Yes. Yes I do want a drink. I want a big drink. And then I think we should talk about why you're calling her Clara.

ANGELICA: Oh! Right. That detail.

ELSA: What did she tell you?

HENRICK: That you're a stalker.

ELSA: I suppose that's true. [*To* HENRICK] Do you know why I'm here?

ANGELICA: You're obsessed with me.

ELSA: [*to* HENRICK, *still aiming the gun at him*] Why don't you ask her? She's right there.

ANGELICA *takes the drink and moves towards* ELSA.

ANGELICA: Cheers.

ELSA *turns to point the pistol at* ANGELICA.

ANGELICA*'s body tenses up. But then,* ANGELICA *relaxes and moves even closer. She stops only when the pistol is centimetres from her face.*

ELSA: I'm her daughter.

ANGELICA: You can't make me love you.

ELSA, *hurt, lowers the pistol. She wipes tears from her eyes.*

HENRICK *takes the opportunity to seize the pistol. He snatches for it. It works. He puts the safety back on.*

Shoot her!

HENRICK: *Angelica.*

ANGELICA: Go on.

HENRICK: [*gentle, reasonable*] *I can't.*

ANGELICA: Give it here then.

HENRICK: You're upset.

ANGELICA: Give me the gun!

ANGELICA *grabs the pistol off* HENRICK.

ANGELICA *approaches* ELSA.

ELSA: GET AWAY FROM ME!

ANGELICA *raises the pistol.*

[*To* HENRICK] STOP HER!

HENRICK: Angelica, don't.

ANGELICA *cocks the pistol.*

ELSA: Maman?!

ANGELICA: DON'T CALL ME THAT!

ELSA: I am thy creature. I ought to be thy Adam.*

ANGELICA: We are strangers.*

ELSA: You, my Creator, detest and spurn me?*

ANGELICA: There can be no relationship between you and me.*

ELSA: You are my maker.*

ANGELICA *grasps the pistol tight. She aims.*

Some destiny of the most horrible kind hangs over us.*

She can't do it.

ANGELICA: Just leave.

She lowers the pistol.

I never want to see you again.

ELSA *nods.*

ELSA *lunges for the pistol, she wrestles it out of* ANGELICA*'s grip. They stay entangled in some way, it's not a clean handover.*

You love me?

ELSA: Yes.

ANGELICA: Then don't do this.

ELSA: I'm sorry.

ANGELICA: No-one has to die tonight.

ELSA: That's not how it ends for us.

ANGELICA: We can both walk out alive.

ELSA *grips the pistol tighter.*

ELSA: Farewell, Frankenstein.*

ANGELICA *braces, but then* ELSA *turns the pistol on herself. She fires.*

Blackout.

In blackout:

ANNA: Oh my God. Oh my God!

MARGOT: Stay in it. This is great. Keep rolling.

FIRST AD: Still rolling!

Then lights up on:

HENRICK: Are you alright? Did she hurt you?

ANNA: Can you breathe? Can you talk?

HENRICK: Do you know her?

ANNA: Call an ambulance.

HENRICK *doesn't move.*

HENRICK: I will. Just tell me what's going on.

ANNA: Henrick?

HENRICK: You can trust me.

ANNA: *Please.*

HENRICK: Just tell me what's really going on here and I'll call an ambulance.

ANNA: … I don't know.

HENRICK: No, no I think you're lying.

ESTÉE: [*a gurgling sound*] Mmmm.

ANNA: She's breathing. She needs an actual doctor.

ESTÉE: [*a gurgling sound*] Mmmm.

HENRICK *goes to the prop phone on the desk.*

ANNA: For fuck's sake. Get your actual phone, and call a real ambulance and tell them there's been an accident.

HENRICK *picks up the prop phone and listens for a dial tone. Nothing. Because it's a prop.*

HENRICK: The line's dead.

Then, after a horrible moment, ESTÉE*'s last breath leaves her and she dies.*

ANNA: Oh shit. I think she might've—

HENRICK: Darling?

ANNA: It was an accident.

HENRICK: Come away from her now.

ANNA: The film. My career.

HENRICK: Move away from her.

ANNA: When people find out a girl died, it's going to get really bad.

HENRICK: I mean, this is pretty bad.

ANNA: Well, it's going to get badder!

HENRICK: Why?

ANNA: *Because it's my fault.*

HENRICK: She's dead. She can't hurt you.

ANNA: … She's part of the story now. She's inserted herself into the narrative.

HENRICK: They'll forget her. In time she'll be no-one.

ANNA: I don't think so.

HENRICK: Your films stand alone.

ANNA: Not anymore.

Lightning.

MARGOT: And cut!

The sound stage bell rings.

ANNA *and* HUGH *return to their American accents.* ESTÉE *doesn't move.*

That was brilliant, Anna. You gave me goosebumps.

ANNA: I have the shakes. Look.

MARGOT: Great work, you three.

HUGH: Estée, we've cut.

ANNA: She's dead.

Beat.

She shot herself. You saw it, right?

Beat.

MARGOT: Oh my God!
HUGH: Oh, fuck!

MARGOT *feels for a pulse. Nothing.*

ANNA: I'm sorry, Margot.
MARGOT: What happened?
ANNA: I don't know. I mean, obviously I don't know.
MARGOT: [*calling out*] Call nine-nine-nine.
MEDIC: Calling nine-nine-nine.
ANNA: I thought you knew?
MARGOT: *Wait, you knew?*
ANNA: No! Maybe.
MARGOT: Maybe?
ANNA: It got a bit blurred with the gun.
MARGOT: The gun.

Beat.

HUGH: [*realising*] It was loaded.
ANNA: She must have loaded it.
HUGH: Why would she do that?
ANNA: To make it real.
HUGH: No, that's, that's unhinged.
ANNA: Clearly she was unhinged.
HUGH: I feel sick.
ANNA: That's what I've been telling you. She's been scaring me.
MEDIC: Emergency crew ETA three minutes.
ANNA: [*realising*] We haven't finished pickups.

Pause.

We still need to do them, don't we?
HUGH: Anna. Stop talking.
ANNA: If we're finishing it. I mean, we can not finish it. In which case we stop.

HUGH: Shut the fuck up, Anna.
MARGOT: Everyone just hang tight.
ANNA: If we stop the film will never— *I'm sorry,* I meant to say it's a tragedy. No-one will see her work.

Sirens in the distance.

Finishing pickups would sort of honour that, wouldn't it?

Sirens in the distance.

Don't you think it would be, like, really respectful to finish?
HUGH: [*leading* ANNA *away*] Anna, just chill and take a seat, yeah?

ANNA *sits in silence.*

ANNA: I've seen movies that were released posthumously.
HUGH: …
ANNA: Do you think it'll get shown?

HUGH *shrugs.*

At all?

HUGH *shrugs.*

Ever?!

HUGH *shrugs.*

MEDIC: Emergency crew on set. Everyone out of the way.
ANNA: We have to finish it. It's the right thing to do. Margot? Margot?! Otherwise it'll just stop in the middle—

Blackout.

Then, softly illuminated, from the darkness enters THE PLAYWRIGHT. *She claps slowly a few times.*

PLAYWRIGHT: Okay. Okay. Should we do notes?

The American thriller world dissolves and swirls into …

END OF PART TWO

PART THREE

SCENE SEVEN

We are now on a theatre stage. It's the final dress run the evening before the first preview of a new play. This world is distinctly 'Australian'. It's naturalistic. Self-conscious. The actors now speak in their authentic accents.

ANNA *is now* ACTOR 1, *the actor playing the role of* ANNA.

ESTÉE *is now* ACTOR 2, *the actor playing the role of* ESTÉE.

MARGOT *is now* ACTOR 3, *the actor playing the role of* MARGOT.

HUGH *is now* THE DIRECTOR, *the theatre director of the 'play' we just watched.*

A fifth person enters the frame: THE PLAYWRIGHT. *She's visibly pregnant.*

Depending on staging, during the following ACTOR 1, ACTOR 2 *and* ACTOR 3 *may grab their scripts, water bottles, jumpers and make their way backstage to get out of 'costume' before doing notes.*

DIRECTOR: So. Final dress. What did you think?
PLAYWRIGHT: I took some notes.
DIRECTOR: The sound cues were a bit off tonight.
PLAYWRIGHT: Yeah, at times it seemed a bit jerky.
DIRECTOR: The operator's a moron. She'll get it though. Don't worry.
PLAYWRIGHT: Cool.

Pause.

So should I just?
DIRECTOR: Just?
PLAYWRIGHT: Go through my notes.
DIRECTOR: [*charming, almost flirtatious*] You love it, right?
PLAYWRIGHT: I'm still processing it.
DIRECTOR: But you love it.
PLAYWRIGHT: I'm still processing it. So, sorry in advance if any of these aren't articulated well.

DIRECTOR: You don't love it?

PLAYWRIGHT: …

DIRECTOR: Why did you pause?

PLAYWRIGHT: Okay, so we're jumping straight into notes then.

DIRECTOR: Sure.

PLAYWRIGHT: Do you need to get a notebook or your script or something?

DIRECTOR: Why?

PLAYWRIGHT: To write them down.

DIRECTOR: Hey. Breathe.

PLAYWRIGHT: I'm breathing.

DIRECTOR: You seem a little …

PLAYWRIGHT: A little what?

DIRECTOR: Tense.

He exaggeratedly breathes in and out, indicating she should join him.

PLAYWRIGHT: You cut the final scene.

DIRECTOR: We didn't need it.

PLAYWRIGHT: It feels like it ends really abruptly.

DIRECTOR: It's more interesting, right?

PLAYWRIGHT: …

DIRECTOR: I think it's more interesting.

PLAYWRIGHT: But is it enough?

DIRECTOR: It leaves more unanswered.

PLAYWRIGHT: Are you sure it can, just, stop like that?

DIRECTOR: I think so.

PLAYWRIGHT: But is it saying enough?

DIRECTOR: I think it says a lot.

PLAYWRIGHT: I just felt like in our chats we were really fucking reaching for something.

DIRECTOR: Mate, it's ambitious.

PLAYWRIGHT: … Can we please try putting the scene back in?

He makes a face that says he doesn't want to.

It says more with it there.

DIRECTOR: It already says a lot. If anything the audience will be relieved it doesn't drag on.

PLAYWRIGHT: I didn't think the final scene 'dragged on'.

DIRECTOR: That's because you wrote it.

PLAYWRIGHT: So find a way to direct it that doesn't do that.

DIRECTOR: I did. The solution was to cut it.

PLAYWRIGHT: …

DIRECTOR: It's not personal. Most plays these days are like twenty minutes too long.

PLAYWRIGHT: Because our attention spans are cooked.

DIRECTOR: Exactly. So let's get in, then get out.

PLAYWRIGHT: So theatre *as an entire art form* should pander to that?

DIRECTOR: … It's better with the cut.

PLAYWRIGHT: You don't think ending it with a dead girl is kinda horrible?

DIRECTOR: It's what you wrote.

PLAYWRIGHT: It leaves it in a really dark place.

DIRECTOR: It's a dark story.

PLAYWRIGHT: *Yeah, but.*

DIRECTOR: The creature and its maker are destroyed by each other in the end. That's the story.

PLAYWRIGHT: And you're happy ending it with like, a dead girl? And a woman pushed to psychological breaking point? And an industry of exploitation that isn't held accountable?

DIRECTOR: Oh God, this is going to take longer than five minutes, isn't it?

PLAYWRIGHT: I don't feel comfortable leaving it so disempowered.

DIRECTOR: That's what it was always building to.

PLAYWRIGHT: But once Anna becomes the monster, we need to see her come to her senses, and feel remorse, and learn something about herself.

DIRECTOR: That's boring.

PLAYWRIGHT: It's empowering.

DIRECTOR: Not mutually exclusive.

PLAYWRIGHT: So what are we saying if we leave it like that?

DIRECTOR: What the original was saying.

PLAYWRIGHT: I'm realising I don't want that. It's upsetting.

DIRECTOR: It's an upsetting story. Why do you feel the need to change it?

PLAYWRIGHT: Because of what it says about me as a writer.

DIRECTOR: About *you*?

PLAYWRIGHT: Yes.

DIRECTOR: It's not about you.

PLAYWRIGHT: My name's on it.

DIRECTOR: That doesn't mean it says anything about you.

PLAYWRIGHT: You know what I mean.

DIRECTOR: No. Stop centering yourself. The meaning of the entire piece isn't located in you.

PLAYWRIGHT: If it ends in total chaos, that ultimately says something about how I see creation.

DIRECTOR: Why are you trying to be clever?

PLAYWRIGHT: We're all trying to be clever.

DIRECTOR: I'm not. I'm trying to entertain. No-one cares how smart the ending is. Just write something good.

PLAYWRIGHT *considers, but then disagrees.*

PLAYWRIGHT: … I'm sorry but I feel physically sick to my stomach thinking about it existing in the world with that ending.

DIRECTOR: That's just nerves.

PLAYWRIGHT: It's more than nerves.

DIRECTOR: *They're gonna love it.* The chaos of creation, Anna's downfall: it all makes sense.

PLAYWRIGHT: Okay, while we're talking about Anna. What was with all that extra dialogue when she's waiting for the ambulance?

DIRECTOR: What about it?

PLAYWRIGHT: The character's meant to stay silent but the actor keeps talking.

DIRECTOR: It's more cathartic, right?

PLAYWRIGHT: It's not in the draft.

DIRECTOR: The actors were doing some improv around that moment and discovered it on the floor.

PLAYWRIGHT: Okay.

DIRECTOR: It's helping her keep the momentum through to the final minute.

PLAYWRIGHT: I'll have to script it tonight if it's gonna be in there tomorrow.

DIRECTOR: You don't like the lines?

PLAYWRIGHT: It's not that: it's just if they're the last lines of the play, and I didn't even write them …

DIRECTOR: They were doing impulse work and your dialogue—your beautiful dialogue by the way—*was* the impulse. So there's an emotional connectedness.

PLAYWRIGHT: I just wouldn't put together dialogue like that.

DIRECTOR: I didn't notice it, to be honest.

PLAYWRIGHT: It's clunky, but I can smooth it over.

DIRECTOR: Sure.

PLAYWRIGHT: If it's staying.

DIRECTOR: Yep.

PLAYWRIGHT: Okay, great. I'll send those pages through.

DIRECTOR: Great chat.

PLAYWRIGHT: There's more.

> ACTOR 3 (MARGOT) *walks through the theatre space, out of costume. She's now in cycling gear and carries a bike helmet and a light. Her backpack is slung over her shoulder. She's ready to leave.*

DIRECTOR: Brava, brava!

ACTOR 3: Yeah?

DIRECTOR: *Yeah.*

ACTOR 3: That felt like a weird run.

DIRECTOR: No, it was good.

ACTOR 3: Okay, good. Are you gonna stick around?

DIRECTOR: Let's do notes in the bar.

ACTOR 3: I'm grabbing a beer. You want one?

DIRECTOR: Let me get my wallet.

> THE DIRECTOR *exits briefly to get his wallet, leaving* THE PLAYWRIGHT *and* ACTOR 3 *alone.*

> *They smile at each other.*

ACTOR 3: Hi. I'm one of the actors.

PLAYWRIGHT: I know.

> *Pause.*

PLAYWRIGHT: Congratulations on tonight.

ACTOR 3: Thanks … Thank you.

> *Pause.*

Sorry, we know each other right?

PLAYWRIGHT: I'm the playwright.

ACTOR 3: Oh! Shit!

PLAYWRIGHT: I was in the room for the first weeks of rehearsals.

ACTOR 3: Yeah I remember. Sorry.

PLAYWRIGHT: It's fine.

ACTOR 3: My brain's a bit melted after that run.

PLAYWRIGHT: All good.

ACTOR 3: Was your hair different?

PLAYWRIGHT: No.

ACTOR 3: Different length or something?

PLAYWRIGHT: No, it's the same

ACTOR 3: Oh wait, you've been sick, right?

PLAYWRIGHT: Yeah. That's why I haven't been able to—

ACTOR 3: *We've been so worried.*

PLAYWRIGHT: Thank you, that's so kind.

ACTOR 3: Thoughts and prayers.

PLAYWRIGHT: That's why I haven't been here as much as I would have wanted.

ACTOR 3: Well it's nice to meet you, or see you, I mean.

Pause.

PLAYWRIGHT: You also did that reading of mine at Griffin, like, two years ago? You played the Centrelink staffer.

ACTOR 3: Oh yeah! I remember that.

PLAYWRIGHT: Yeah.

ACTOR 3: Did that play ever—?

PLAYWRIGHT: Ah / no.

ACTOR 3: Get up somewhere?

PLAYWRIGHT: No, it didn't.

ACTOR 3: Damn. They seemed really interested.

PLAYWRIGHT: Yeah they were. They were for a bit there.

ACTOR 3: …

PLAYWRIGHT: Congrats again on your performance tonight.

ACTOR 3: [*genuine, loves compliments*] *Thank you.*

PLAYWRIGHT: …

ACTOR 3: Congrats to you, too.

PLAYWRIGHT: Thank you.

ACTOR 3: On the baby.

PLAYWRIGHT: Oh. Well, / yeah …

ACTOR 3: So what are you writing at the moment?

PLAYWRIGHT: This.

THE DIRECTOR *re-enters. He tosses his wallet to* ACTOR 3. *She catches it.*

DIRECTOR: Tell the others I'll be five.

ACTOR 3: [*to* PLAYWRIGHT] Nice seeing you again.

ACTOR 3 *leaves.*

PLAYWRIGHT: Hey, so I know I've been absent.

DIRECTOR: Totally understand.

PLAYWRIGHT: But I've been in and out of hospital, vomiting my guts out.

DIRECTOR: It sounded awful.

PLAYWRIGHT: You know Mary Shelley was pregnant around the time she wrote *Frankenstein.*

DIRECTOR: Oh wow.

PLAYWRIGHT: But you would know that from all the research you did.

DIRECTOR: Yes. From the research, for the play.

PLAYWRIGHT: This baby is sucking the life out of me.

DIRECTOR: Theresa had terrible morning sickness too.

PLAYWRIGHT: It's worse than morning sickness.

DIRECTOR: She was pretty sick.

PLAYWRIGHT: Hyperemesis. It's a medical condition.

DIRECTOR: It's not a competition.

PLAYWRIGHT: It's potentially life-threatening.

DIRECTOR: You always have to win, don't you?

PLAYWRIGHT: Point is, I know I've been absent, but I should have been consulted if you were gonna change stuff.

DIRECTOR: I don't think I 'changed stuff'.

PLAYWRIGHT: The script is different.

DIRECTOR: A few tiny tweaks.

PLAYWRIGHT: Exactly.

DIRECTOR: That you would have made if you were in the room.

PLAYWRIGHT: [*awkwardly, under her breath*] *Well the contract says 'no changes to the script'.*

DIRECTOR: I think it's actually 'changes need to be requested in writing'.
PLAYWRIGHT: Did I get them in writing?
DIRECTOR: You were in hospital. It wasn't appropriate.
PLAYWRIGHT: I would have wanted to be consulted.
DIRECTOR: Well I didn't assume that, because emailing you when I knew you were in hospital would have been fucking inappropriate.
PLAYWRIGHT: Now you know.
DIRECTOR: I'll take it on board for next time.

Beat.

PLAYWRIGHT: [*hurt*] We've been working on this for years.
DIRECTOR: It's been a great collaboration.
PLAYWRIGHT: I think so too.
DIRECTOR: That's why we got you in. [*Gesturing to their connection*] Because of what this might be.
PLAYWRIGHT: I didn't think a few weeks off rehearsal erases that?
DIRECTOR: A month. When it really mattered. But no. It doesn't.
PLAYWRIGHT: I put so much into it.
DIRECTOR: And now you need to let the work be what it is.
PLAYWRIGHT: No. My work can't just 'be'. It has to 'be good'.

Slow beat. THE DIRECTOR *nods, he understands she's hurt.*

DIRECTOR: So what would you change?
PLAYWRIGHT: Really?
DIRECTOR: Go on.
PLAYWRIGHT: Text-wise or performance-wise?
DIRECTOR: I don't see a separation.
PLAYWRIGHT: In that case, it's actually the whole thing.
DIRECTOR: What about it?
PLAYWRIGHT: The whole thing is …

She can't say it.

Okay, example: can we please completely restage the opening?
DIRECTOR: What do you mean 'restage'?
PLAYWRIGHT: The fog element.
DIRECTOR: That's my vision for that moment.
PLAYWRIGHT: It's not the right atmosphere.
DIRECTOR: That's my vision.

PLAYWRIGHT: What's it serving though?

DIRECTOR: The text.

PLAYWRIGHT: Is it?

DIRECTOR: When I read your play, what drew me in was a vision of this psychological, gothic haze. That's always been part of the bigger picture for me. This big theatrical image that doesn't make sense logically if you were to deconstruct it. But *emotionally*, for an audience, they know it's the right choice.

PLAYWRIGHT: … It's atmospheric but I'm not sure it's doing anything.

DIRECTOR: You'll feel it tomorrow. When this room is full of people, you'll feel it.

PLAYWRIGHT: *It's really a lot.*

DIRECTOR: It's meant to be a lot.

PLAYWRIGHT: It seems very obvious.

DIRECTOR: An audience won't see it like that.

PLAYWRIGHT: See it like what?

DIRECTOR: The way you're seeing it. It's impossible for you to see it the way an audience would.

PLAYWRIGHT: Maybe.

DIRECTOR: You're watching it tonight, final dress, fearful, tentative. The way a parent watches their child run around a playground.

PLAYWRIGHT: I don't think I am.

DIRECTOR: You think your play is so precious and delicate and special and we need to be very careful with it. But no, we don't. You don't need to hold the audience's hand and have them like and understand the whole thing. You can take some risks. Make some bold choices to elevate it.

PLAYWRIGHT: Then maybe the actors don't get it or something.

DIRECTOR: Don't blame the actors.

PLAYWRIGHT: Because the moment's not translating.

DIRECTOR: The actors get it. What I've asked them to do is react *against* it. To add contrast. It's all in the text.

THE DIRECTOR *makes a show of finding his script to make reference.*

Scene One, Angelica says— [*Reading*] 'Even for an adaptation. I still have to find a point of entry; my own empathy or parallels.'

What's really clever about that moment is the complexity. You can read it multiple ways.

PLAYWRIGHT: Yeah, I wrote it.

DIRECTOR: Her next line— [*Reading*] 'It's not art imitating life, it's art imitating itself.'

PLAYWRIGHT: I wrote that one too.

DIRECTOR: So it's important we don't draw too much attention to the very subtle, very gentle nod to metatheatre, because otherwise—

PLAYWRIGHT: For me it actually *is* really important—

DIRECTOR: It's important to me too. Of course.

PLAYWRIGHT: Yeah, but for me personally—

DIRECTOR: Well, this work is bigger than you. Bigger than both of us.

PLAYWRIGHT: That's true.

DIRECTOR: Smarter than us perhaps.

PLAYWRIGHT: My play is smarter than me?

DIRECTOR: In ways. You see what's really clever about that sequence is—

PLAYWRIGHT: You don't need to explain the scene to me; I literally wrote it.

DIRECTOR: The audience will understand my vision. Even if you don't. They'll get it. I'm creating space for their personal projections. Leaving pieces unresolved. So they can decide what it means to them.

PLAYWRIGHT: I don't want them to do that.

DIRECTOR: You can't really control how they interpret it.

PLAYWRIGHT: We can a bit.

DIRECTOR: Not really.

PLAYWRIGHT: I think we can.

DIRECTOR: That's not how I make work.

PLAYWRIGHT: No, no, that's right.

DIRECTOR: I don't spoon-feed my audience, sorry, I respect them more than that.

PLAYWRIGHT: No, you usually work with dead male playwrights so you don't have to have a two-way conversation.

DIRECTOR: *Wow.*

PLAYWRIGHT: Interpret the classics however you want. Bend the text to your agenda. But this is new work.

DIRECTOR: *You wrote an adaptation.*

PLAYWRIGHT: It's a complete reimagining.
DIRECTOR: Ah ah ah, you wrote an adaptation.
PLAYWRIGHT: So what?
DIRECTOR: I'm interpreting your adaptation alongside the original.
PLAYWRIGHT: Yeah that's cool, ignore the author's intention.
DIRECTOR: Well, there are technically two authors for this work.
PLAYWRIGHT: Well one of them is DEAD and the other thinks you're a WANKER.
DIRECTOR: Then don't write an adaptation next time.
PLAYWRIGHT: I didn't have a choice!
DIRECTOR: Why?
PLAYWRIGHT: [*gesturing to the theatre*] That's the only way you can get something on here!
DIRECTOR: Have I hit a nerve?
PLAYWRIGHT: Oh fuck you. I helped you with so many of your shitty Chekhov translations.
DIRECTOR: Wow, tell me what you really think.
PLAYWRIGHT: It's so you. The whole thing is so you that I can't even hear my voice in it.
DIRECTOR: They're saying every single line you wrote.
PLAYWRIGHT: No, you've inserted yourself into it somehow. Into the subtext.
DIRECTOR: I think you're seeing something that isn't there.
PLAYWRIGHT: You literally cast yourself in it. It's impossible not to see you.
DIRECTOR: It's still your play.
PLAYWRIGHT: And I hate what you've done with it!
DIRECTOR: That's a pretty awful thing to say.

A painful beat.

The mood's changed now.

PLAYWRIGHT: Say something.

Pause.

DIRECTOR: I'm really hurt you'd say that.
PLAYWRIGHT: Sorry.
DIRECTOR: It's honestly quite hurtful to be attacked so personally.

PLAYWRIGHT: It wasn't a personal attack.

DIRECTOR: You 'hate what I've done with it'? I was really excited to do this with you.

PLAYWRIGHT: I was too.

Pause.

DIRECTOR: Can you just … tell me the opposite.

PLAYWRIGHT: What?

DIRECTOR: That you love it, it's even better than your original conception, so I can get the team through previews, through opening night, and into the season.

She stays silent.

I need you to tell me you love it.

She stays silent.

You don't have to mean it. I just need to hear you say it.

PLAYWRIGHT: Why?

DIRECTOR: Because I'm trying.

PLAYWRIGHT: The way you've brought it to life is completely wrong.

DIRECTOR: You haven't been here to nurture it, so this is what it is now.

PLAYWRIGHT: I'm actually feeling a bit embarrassed my name's on it.

DIRECTOR: I think it's good.

PLAYWRIGHT: It's not.

DIRECTOR: Its essence is good. It's trying to be good. You need to be willing to see it that way.

PLAYWRIGHT: No, if that's what you're putting in front of people, then no, I don't think it's very good.

DIRECTOR: Fine. You hate it. Fine. But you need to put on a smile, and walk into that bar, look those actors in the eye, and tell them they're doing great.

PLAYWRIGHT: I can't do that.

DIRECTOR: Because otherwise you're going to rock their confidence before opening night. You need to be a professional right now.

PLAYWRIGHT: I am being professional.

DIRECTOR: No, you're being selfish.

PLAYWRIGHT: I'm being honest.

DIRECTOR: And now you're being confrontational.

PLAYWRIGHT: What's so confrontational about being honest?

DIRECTOR: It's a confrontational vibe and it's unsafe.

PLAYWRIGHT: Why is it unsafe to express a different artistic opinion?

DIRECTOR: I've listened to your opinion, I'm / listening!

PLAYWRIGHT: So do something more than / listen!

DIRECTOR: Enough! I love you. But this is why you don't turn up at final dress with notes.

PLAYWRIGHT: I was literally hospitalised.

DIRECTOR: And we're so relieved you're feeling better now.

PLAYWRIGHT: I'm well within my rights to give you notes.

DIRECTOR: And I've listened to your notes. And as the director of this production, I've decided I'm leaving it as is. We'll see where it lands after preview.

PLAYWRIGHT: …

DIRECTOR: So now might be time for you to get some rest, huh? So you're fresh.

PLAYWRIGHT: If that's what you put up, we're not going into previews tomorrow.

DIRECTOR: Don't be so dramatic.

PLAYWRIGHT: If you don't get those actors back in here to workshop those scenes, then there isn't going to be a production at all.

DIRECTOR: Are you serious?

PLAYWRIGHT: I will literally call my agent right now and pull the rights.

DIRECTOR: For real? Wait, are you even allowed to do that?

PLAYWRIGHT: The contract is, 'No changes to the text.'

DIRECTOR: We're friends.

PLAYWRIGHT: Are we?

DIRECTOR: I was at your wedding.

PLAYWRIGHT: A lot of people were at my wedding.

DIRECTOR: I contributed to your honeymoon fund.

PLAYWRIGHT: Do you remember what happened on my honeymoon?

DIRECTOR: Should I?

PLAYWRIGHT: I was in Santorini and you emailed to say this show was on the slate all of a sudden, and I had three nights to get you new pages.

DIRECTOR: In hindsight, that wasn't great timing.

PLAYWRIGHT: Oh my God, why are we talking about this?!

DIRECTOR: You brought it up.

PLAYWRIGHT: I DON'T WANT TO TALK ABOUT THIS!

Beat.

DIRECTOR: [*gentle*] Hey, hey, hey. You're allowed to be freaked out. You've got a lot going on.

She tries to figure it out.

PLAYWRIGHT: [*finding the solution*] Okay … So … We're riffing on this epic story about someone who believes they're destined for greatness.

DIRECTOR: Uh-huh.

PLAYWRIGHT: And they create a new human. But the thing is, no-one wants new humans. They have perfectly good humans. They don't need him cobbling together dead body parts to make something new, when they're perfectly happy with the humans that already exist. But he makes it anyway. And he knows it's horrible as soon as it's made. And it ruins his life. But you can't know whether what you're making is good or bad until it's out there. And all along, the whole time, his friends, his mentors, his parents, his fiancée—people who loved him—were telling him to stop. Literally stop. Don't lock yourself in your room. Don't dig up the dead. Don't make new things.

DIRECTOR: And you're getting to your point, which is—?

PLAYWRIGHT: I guess my point is, if I had to sum it up—

DIRECTOR: Yes, *please*—

PLAYWRIGHT: When what you have to offer the world is horrible and yet the drive you feel to create it is God-like … what's anyone meant to do with that impulse?

DIRECTOR: [*considering*] Well, he sets out to destroy what he created, doesn't he?

PLAYWRIGHT: Yes.

DIRECTOR: Before it destroys him.

The theatrical-ness of this world makes itself known. THE DIRECTOR *notices this change.*

PLAYWRIGHT: I'm sorry, but I need to, I need to

DIRECTOR: [*noticing the world shifting*] Okay, pause. This is getting— [*Afraid of the distortion*] I think maybe something hormonal is going on?

PLAYWRIGHT: Oh, how woke of you to suggest this is all hormonal.

DIRECTOR: *Pregnancy* hormones, not *menstrual* hormones.
PLAYWRIGHT: Are you actually defending yourself?
DIRECTOR: Yes. When Theresa was pregnant she was a fucking nightmare.
PLAYWRIGHT: I'm sorry, but I need to, I need to destroy it.

The world begins to distort.

DIRECTOR: No. Wait!
PLAYWRIGHT: Before it destroys me.
DIRECTOR: Don't do this. Please. You worked for years on it.
PLAYWRIGHT: I hate it.
DIRECTOR: People might love it.
PLAYWRIGHT: It's monstrous.
DIRECTOR: So you get to decide it can't exist?
PLAYWRIGHT: I wrote it.
DIRECTOR: It's bigger than you now.
PLAYWRIGHT: I made it, I have the right to destroy it.
DIRECTOR: I can't let you do that.
PLAYWRIGHT: I want it dead!

The theatre set collapses in on itself.

DIRECTOR: No. We're not deconstructing this again.
PLAYWRIGHT: Why shouldn't I?
DIRECTOR: We're past that! Who cares what the author thinks?

Lightning. The beginning of a tempest.

PLAYWRIGHT: Do you know how hard it is to write a play? Do you know what it costs? The pound of flesh we expect artists to give every single time?
DIRECTOR: That's the deal though, isn't it? Always has been.
PLAYWRIGHT: Even if it destroys the person giving it?
DIRECTOR: So stop giving it.
PLAYWRIGHT: Because companies won't touch it unless I can point to my exact pound of flesh, and locate it in the play, and articulate exactly why I should be the one to write it.
DIRECTOR: Then don't make work that way.
PLAYWRIGHT: I don't know how not to.
DIRECTOR: Just take the commission and make something.
PLAYWRIGHT: I don't make things like that.

DIRECTOR: Take the commission and make something. Then take the next opportunity. And make the next thing. Then make the next thing. And then make the next. And when you're all out of things to make, I guess you're done here.

PLAYWRIGHT: Keep producing and producing and producing and producing?

DIRECTOR: Pretty much.

PLAYWRIGHT: To what end?

DIRECTOR: There is no end to creation. It keeps going and going and going.

PLAYWRIGHT: That's not how I write. It means so much. It matters so much.

Beat.

DIRECTOR: It's just a play.

PLAYWRIGHT: No. The great plays are more than just a play.

DIRECTOR: [*gentle, kind*] So maybe this one isn't great?

Slow beat.

PLAYWRIGHT: I tried.

DIRECTOR: There'll be another one.

Pause.

You hate this one? Oh well.

PLAYWRIGHT: It's just a play?

DIRECTOR: Don't destroy yourself because of it.

PLAYWRIGHT: It's just a play.

DIRECTOR: Tomorrow, try watching it. Be outside it, and look at it, out there in the world, without wishing it dead. Then you have your alternative ending.

Slow beat.

She nods, 'Okay'.

The tempest settles with the PLAYWRIGHT.

Beat.

I better go give notes.

She nods.

You want to join?

PLAYWRIGHT: I might sit a bit.

He nods.

DIRECTOR: [*going to leave*] Can you switch off the workers on your way out?

Just before he exits, he calls back to her in an act of kindness.

Same time tomorrow?

PLAYWRIGHT: Same time tomorrow.

THE DIRECTOR *exits, leaving* THE PLAYWRIGHT *alone.*

For a moment it rains for real. No sound effects or lights like before, but real water; real rain.

THE PLAYWRIGHT *leaves the playing space and watches the world from the outside.*

After a moment, ACTOR 2 *(*ESTÉE*), now out of costume, enters.*

ACTOR 2: Oh great, you're still here!

PLAYWRIGHT: I was just leaving.

ACTOR 2: Did you like it?

Pause.

PLAYWRIGHT: You were brilliant.

ACTOR 2 *beams with pride.*

ACTOR 2: Hey? Can I ask you about this line?

THE PLAYWRIGHT *smiles to say 'go on'.*

ACTOR 2 *raises her script to find the section for* THE PLAYWRIGHT. *She points to a moment.* THE PLAYWRIGHT *nods in recognition. The* PLAYWRIGHT *goes to give her answer as the lights fade on the pair of them.*

THE END